Border Raids and Reivers

by Robert Borland

The object we have had in view in the following pages has been (1) to indicate briefly the causes which produced Border reiving; (2) to show the extent to which the system was ultimately developed; (3) to describe the means adopted by both Governments for its suppression; (4) to illustrate the way in which the *rugging and riving*—to use a well-known phrase—was carried on; (5) to explain how these abnormal conditions were in the end effectually removed; and (6) to set forth in brief outline some of the more prominent traits in the lives and characters of the men who were most closely identified with this extraordinary phase of Border life.

We have to acknowledge our indebtedness for much of the information conveyed in the following pages to Scott's "Border Antiquities" and "Border Minstrelsy," Nicolson's "Leges Marchiarum," Pitcairn's "Criminal Trials," "Calendar of Border Papers" (recently published), "Cary's Memoirs"—Froissart, Godscroft, Pitscottie, Pinkerton—and host of other writers on Border themes.

It is in no spirit of mock-modesty we acknowledge how inadequately the object we have had in view has been realised. The subject is so large and many-sided that we have found it difficult to compress within the compass of a single volume anything like an adequate outline of a theme which is at once so varied and interesting.

In coming to the consideration of this subject, there is one fact which it is well the reader should carefully bear in mind, and that is, that from the peculiar circumstances in which Borderers were placed in early times, the only alternative they had was either to *starve or steal*. The recognition of this fact will at least awaken our sympathy, if it does not always command our approval, when we come to consider the lives and characters of the Border Reivers.

I.

THE AULD ENEMY.

"Near a Border frontier, in the time of war,
There's ne'er a man, but he's a freebooter."—Satchells.

There are few more remarkable phenomena in the political or social life of Scotland than what is familiarly known as "Border Reiving." In olden times it prevailed along the whole line of the Borders from Berwick to the Solway, embracing the counties of Berwick, Roxburgh, Selkirk, Peebles, and Dumfries. During a period of some three or four hundred years these districts were chiefly inhabited by hordes of moss-troopers, who made it the chief business of their lives to harry and despoil their English neighbours. On every convenient opportunity the Scottish reivers crossed the Border, and carried off whatever came readiest to hand—horses, cows, sheep, "insight and outsight," nothing coming amiss to them unless it was either too heavy or too hot. Those on the English side who were thus despoiled were not slow to retaliate, and generally succeeded, to some extent, in making good the losses they sustained. This system of plunder and reprisal ultimately attained an extraordinary development. All classes, from the Chief of the clan to the meanest serf over whom he ruled, were engaged in it. Indeed it must be frankly admitted that the most notorious thieves were often those who had least excuse for indulging in such nefarious practices—gentlemen in high position like the Scotts, Kers, Johnstones, and Maxwells, and who in many cases had been chosen by the Government to repress the reiving propensities of their clans and followers.

Some who have made a superficial acquaintance with this remarkable phase of Border life have rushed to the conclusion that the great Border Chiefs, and those over whom they exercised a kind of patriarchal authority, must have been dowered with a "double dose of original sin." In proof of this it is pointed out that a widely different state of affairs prevailed in other parts of the country, for example in Fife, and the Lothians, and generally speaking, throughout the whole of the west of Scotland, and consequently the only way in which they can account for the singular condition of the Borders is by predicating an essentially lower moral type. We do not believe that this theory, plausible though it may appear, will bear a moment's serious consideration. No doubt among the "broken men" of the Debateable land, and in some parts of Liddesdale, you will find a considerable number of disreputable characters whose only law was the length of their own swords. But it is a mistake to suppose that such individuals represent the general type of the inhabitants of the Borderland. The very fact that these men had no Chief to represent them shows that they had, so to speak, fallen out of the ranks.

The solution of this problem must be sought in another direction. It will be found by a careful study of the history of the country that Border reiving was, to a considerable extent, the result of a concatenation of circumstances over which the inhabitants of these districts had little or no control. They were the victims of an evil fate. It was not merely their proximity to the English Border which occasioned their misdeeds. It is an interesting and significant fact that, till near the close of the 13th century, the Border Counties were as law-abiding as any other part of the realm. Petty skirmishes were, no doubt, of frequent occurrence, as might be expected; but the deep rooted aversion to the English which characterises the subsequent period of Scottish history had hardly at that time any real existence. How the change was brought about will become apparent as we bring under review some salient facts in Scottish history which have a direct and immediate bearing on the question before us.

It must be borne in mind that for a period of more than three hundred years Scotland was kept in a condition of political distraction by the insane desire on the part of the English Government to reduce it to a state of vassalage. When this policy was first determined on everything seemed favourable to its speedy realisation. When Alexander III., a wise and gracious King, under whose reign the country had greatly prospered, was accidentally killed when hunting in the neighbourhood of Kinghorn, the Crown reverted to his grand-daughter, the Maid of Norway, who was then a child of tender years. At this unfortunate juncture Edward I. of England resolved that the two countries should be united under one Sovereign; at least this was the object of his ambition. He was fully convinced that so long as Scotland maintained her political independence, England would have to reckon with a powerful adversary. If he could only succeed, by fair means or foul, in gaining Scotland over as a fief of England, then the country as a whole would enjoy the immunities and benefits naturally accruing to its position as an island. England would thus be in an immensely more advantageous position to resist foreign invasion, and its influence and power as an aggressive force would be indefinitely increased. The object aimed at was an exceedingly desirable one. Unfortunately it was a sane policy insanely pursued. Had the English King only been gifted with more self-restraint, had he but been prepared to wait patiently the natural development of events, and not to have

4

struck the iron *before* it was hot, he might have succeeded in gaining his end, a result which would have changed the whole complexion and current of Scottish history. Whether this would have been better or worse, more to our own advantage and the advantage of Great Britain, as a whole, is one of those points about which there may be considerable difference of opinion. Many have regretted that the Union of the Crowns was not effected in the 14th century rather than in the 17th, as such a consummation would have saved the country much, both of bloodshed and treasure. It may be so. It cannot be denied that from a purely material point of view it might have been better had Scotland gracefully complied with the wishes of Edward. But man cannot live by bread alone. There are higher and better things in the life of a people than mere material well-being, and in view of these it was well that Scotland maintained her independence. The record of her achievements, when contending against the most overwhelming odds, and the example of those heroic personalities, which mark the progress of her history, have been a perennial fountain of inspiration to the Scottish people, have made them what they are. While, therefore, there may be some cause for regret, on the ground of political expediency, that the union of the two countries was so late in being effected, yet on other and higher grounds there is just reason for thankfulness that things took the course they did. What would Scotland have been without its Wallace or Bruce? or what would it have been apart from the long and arduous struggle through which it was destined to pass ere it gained an assured and thoroughly independent political position? The long years of struggle and desolating warfare constitute an important factor in the social and intellectual evolution of the nation. The best qualities of the Scottish character and intellect were developed in the seething maelstrom of political strife and internecine war. It may be that "the course of Providence is also the orbit of wisdom."

Edward in trying to bring Scotland under his sway pursued a two-fold policy. He endeavoured to prevent as far as possible all union among the most powerful Scottish barons. He arrayed their private and selfish ambition against the love of their country. He sowed dissension in their councils, and richly rewarded their treachery. Those who dared to oppose his well-laid schemes were treated with unmitigated severity. His success in this respect was complete. He had the satisfaction of seeing the country torn to pieces by contending factions. His way was now open for applying more drastic measures. He raised a powerful army and invaded Scotland. The town of Berwick was then an important centre of commerce, and he was determined at all hazards to make himself master of the city. "He despatched a large division, with orders to assault the town, choosing a line of march which concealed them from the citizens; and he commanded his fleet to enter the river at the same moment that the great body of the army, led by himself, were ready to storm. The Scottish army fiercely assaulted the ships, burnt three of them, and compelled the rest to retire; but they in their turn were driven back by the fury of the land attack. Edward himself, mounted on horseback, was the first who leaped the dyke; and the soldiers, animated by the example and presence of their King, carried everything before them. All the horrors of a rich and populous city, sacked by an inflamed soldiery, and a commander thirsting for vengeance, now succeeded. *Seventeen thousand persons*, without distinction of age or sex, were put to the sword; and for two days the city ran with blood like a river. The churches, to which the miserable inhabitants fled for sanctuary, were violated and defiled with blood, spoiled of their sacred ornaments, and turned into stables for the English cavalry.".

This ruthless massacre produced a profound sensation all over the country, but more especially on the Borders, and had much to do in creating that bitter feeling of hostility with which the English were ever afterwards regarded. To harass and despoil them was looked upon almost as a sacred duty. This miserable butchery of the inoffensive lieges instantly led to reprisals. Under the Earls of Ross, Menteith, and Athole, the Scottish army crossed the English Border, and ravaged with merciless severity the districts of Redesdale and Tynedale. The monasteries of Lanercost and Hexham were given to the flames, towns and villages destroyed, and the surrounding country laid waste. The Scots returned laden with booty. But the success which had crowned their arms was of doubtful utility. It only served to fan the flame of vengeful ire in the breast of the English King, who now resolved on the complete subjugation of the country. He marched against Dunbar with an army of ten thousand foot, and a thousand heavy armed horse. The Scots opposed his progress with an army much superior in point of numbers, and occupying a position of great strategic importance on the heights above Spot. As the English army had necessarily to deploy in passing along the valley it was supposed that the ranks had somehow fallen into confusion. The Scots precipitately rushed upon the enemy, only to find, to their dismay, that the English army was under the most perfect discipline, and ready for the attack. After a short resistance the Scottish columns were thrown into inextricable confusion, and were routed with great slaughter, leaving ten thousand brave soldiers dead in the field. History has a strange knack of repeating itself. Three hundred and fifty years after, the Scottish covenanters committed a similar blunder at the same place when opposing the progress of Oliver Cromwell, and with an equally disastrous result. The progress of Edward now partook of the nature of a triumphal march. He threw his army upon Edinburgh, and in the course of eight days made himself master of the Castle. He then proceeded to Perth, where he received the submission of Baliol, who seemed anxious to rid himself of an office the duties of which he was constitutionally unfit to discharge. The King continued his march to Aberdeen, and from thence to Elgin, without resistance. The nobles hurried into his presence to tender their submission. With indecent haste they renounced the alliance with Bruce, and took the oath of fealty to the destroyer of their country's liberties. It was a dark and tragic hour in Scottish history.

As Edward returned on his way to Berwick, where he proposed holding a Parliament, he visited Scone, and took with him the "famous and fatal stone" upon which for many ages the Scottish Kings had been crowned and anointed. "This, considered by the Scots as the national Palladium, along with the Scottish Sceptre and Crown, the English monarch placed in the Cathedral of Westminster as an offering to Edward the Confessor, and as a memorial of what he deemed his absolute conquest of Scotland, a conquest which, before a single year elapsed, was entirely wrested from him."

We must now pass rapidly over one of the most eventful and stirring periods of Scottish history, during which Wallace and Bruce, by almost superhuman efforts, succeeded in delivering the country from the domination and control of England. The battle of Bannockburn gave the final blow to the lofty pretensions of the English monarch. He began to realise that the conquest of Scotland was not to be effected so easily as he had at one time vainly thought. But unfortunately this splendid victory did not result in inaugurating a reign of peace and goodwill between the two countries. After all that the Scottish people had suffered at the hands of their enemies, it was impossible for them to remain quiescent. They were determined on revenge. Hence we find that in the early autumn of 1314 Douglas and Edward Bruce were despatched across the eastern march, and ravaged with fire and sword the counties of Northumberland and Durham. They even penetrated into Yorkshire, plundered the town of Richmond, and drove away a large booty of cattle, and made many prisoners. The inhabitants of the north of England were paralysed with fear. Walsingham declares that a hundred Englishmen would not hesitate to fly from two or three Scottish soldiers, so grievously had their wonted courage deserted them.

Another army of Scottish soldiers marched through Redesdale and Tynedale, "marking their progress by the black ashes of the towns and villages."

In the spring of the following year this predatory mode of warfare was again resumed, and Northumberland and the principality of Durham ravaged. A great quantity of plunder was collected, and the inhabitants compelled to redeem their property by paying a high tribute. The army of Bruce seemed invincible, and the northern counties of England were made to pay dearly for the temerity of the king in venturing to challenge the patriotism and prowess of the Scottish people.

These events produced a profound impression on the people as a whole, especially on the dwellers on the Scottish Border. The sacking of Berwick, and the indiscriminate slaughter of its inhabitants, whose only offence was that they refused to open their gates to the usurper, were not soon forgotten, and engendered in the Border mind an undying hatred of England. It is not to be wondered at that the inhabitants of the Scottish Border should seldom either think or speak of the English except as their "auld enemies." To despoil them became, if not a religious, at least a patriotic duty. These circumstances to which reference has been made, and others of a kindred nature, may account, in some degree at least, for the extraordinary fact that the Border mosstrooper never seems to have been ashamed of his calling. On the contrary he gloried in it. In his eyes it was honourable and worthy. The undaunted bearing of the Bold Buccleuch, for example, and his cavalier manner in dealing with the English wardens, showed how thoroughly he enjoyed the work in which he was engaged. Eure tells how, on one occasion, he sent his cousin, Henry Bowes, to confer with this famous freebooter on some question in dispute, but Buccleuch "scorned to speak with him, and gathered his forces; and if my said cousin had not wisely foreseen and taken time to have come away he had been stayed himself. Two several messages were sent from Buccleuch from out his company that were in the field, part to have stayed with him and those that were with him. Not long since some of his men having stolen in my March, my men following their trade were stayed of his officer of Hermitage, their horses taken and themselves escaped on foot."

The English warden had evidently considerable difficulty in accounting for Buccleuch's attitude, for we find in a letter written to Burghley a few days after this happened that he is disposed to attribute his enmity to England to his zeal for Romanism. "His secret friends," he says, "say he is a papist; his surest friends in court are papists about the Queen, and labour his grace with the King. He strengthened himself much of late, and secretly says he will not stir till some certainty of the Spaniards arrive. To England he is a secret enemy, mighty proud, publishing his descent to be from Angus, and laboureth to be created Earl, and claimeth his blood to be partly royal. His poverty is great, all which concurring with his pride and Spanish religion, I leave to your honourable wisdom to censure."

This picture is certainly painted in strong colours. The one point in it which is really significant, however, is that Buccleuch was "a secret enemy to England." This may be said of nine-tenths of the Border reivers. It was not the mere love of plunder or mischief which impelled them to prosecute their calling. They were animated by a spirit of revenge. Times almost without number the armies of England had crossed the Border, burning villages and homesteads, destroying the crops, carrying off goods and cattle, leaving those whom they had thus ruthlessly despoiled to the tender mercies of an uncertain climate and an impoverished soil, from which even at the best they had difficulty in extracting a bare subsistence.

The English were, comparatively speaking, rich and powerful. They could command great forces, against which it was in vain, in most cases, for the Scottish Borderers to contend. Hence when they were assailed they drove their cattle into the recesses of mountain or forest, burned or otherwise destroyed what they could not remove—so that the enemy might be enriched as little as possible—and betook themselves to some distant shelter, where they awaited the course of events. As soon as the enemy had withdrawn, they returned to their places of abode, which, though destroyed, were easily reconstructed—the work of rebuilding being done in a day or two—and then they set about recouping themselves for the losses they had sustained by making incursions on the English Border, and carrying off every thing they could lay their hands on. This system of plunder and reprisal went on merrily along the whole line of the Borders for many generations. All the great Border families were involved in it, and devoted themselves to the work with a zeal and enthusiasm which left nothing to be desired. They doubtless felt that in plundering the English they were not only enriching themselves, but promoting the interests of their country, and paying back a long standing and heavily accumulating debt.

<hr>

II.

PERCY'S PENNON.

"It fell about the Lammas time
When Yeomen wonne their hay,
The doughty Douglas 'gan to ride
In England to take a prey."

Battle of Otterburn.

he Battle of Otterburn, which took place in the autumn of 1388, is without question one of the most interesting episodes in Border history, and is especially significant as an illustration of the prowess and chivalry of the Border Chiefs. The chief combatants on the Scottish side were the Earls of Douglas, Moray, March, and Crawford, the Lord Montgomery, and Patrick Hepburn of Hales, and his son. On the English side were Sir Henry (Hotspur) and Sir Ralph Percy, sons of the Earl of Northumberland; the Seneschal of York, Sir Ralph Langley, Sir Matthew Redman, governor of Berwick, Sir Robert Ogle, Sir Thomas Grey, Sir Thomas Hatton, Sir John Felton, Sir John Lillburne, Sir William Walsingham, and many others, all good men and true. The circumstances which brought about this famous encounter are worth recalling, as they shed an interesting light on the history of the period, as well as on the manners and customs of the age. The Scots, with the aid of their French allies, under the command of Sir John de Vienne, had made frequent successful incursions upon the English Borders, ravaging with fire and sword considerable districts of the country, both to the east and west of the frontier. This naturally led to retaliating expeditions. At last the state of affairs became so desperate that the young King, Richard II., determined to invade Scotland, and mete out summary punishment on the depredators. An army of extraordinary power and splendour was assembled; and the King, attended by his uncles and all the principal nobles of the kingdom, set out for the Scottish Border. If he expected to reap a rich harvest of booty by this invasion of the Scottish kingdom he was doomed to bitter disappointment. As he passed through Liddesdale and Teviotdale at the head of his army he found that the country had been cleared of everything that could be conveniently carried off. The cattle had been driven into the forest and mountain fastnesses; all the goods and chattels had been secured in places of safety; nothing was left but the green crops, and these being trampled upon were rendered practically worthless. But most wonderful of all—he never

8

could come within sight of the enemy! The whole region through which he passed was lonely and desolate as a wilderness. The reason of this was that the French and Scots forces had fallen back upon Berwick, the commander of the Scots army being unwilling to hazard the fate of the country by an encounter with such an overwhelmingly superior force. The French commander, De Vienne, was impatient, and bitterly disappointed at not being permitted to attack the invaders. The Earl of Douglas, in order to demonstrate the hopelessness of an encounter, conveyed him to a lofty eminence, commanding a mountain pass through which the English army was at that moment defiling, and where unseen themselves, they could see its imposing array. The Scottish leader pointed out the number and discipline of the men-at-arms, and the superiority of the equipments of the archers, and then asked the French Knight whether he could recommend the Scots to encounter such a numerous and completely accoutred army with a few ill-trained Highland bowmen, and their light-armed prickers mounted on little hackneys. He could not but admit the risk was too great. "But yet," said he, "if you do not give the English battle they will destroy your country." "Let them do their worst," replied Douglas, "they will find but little to destroy. Our people have all retired into the mountains and forests, and have carried off their flocks and herds and household stuff along with them. We will surround them with a desert, and while they never see an enemy they shall never stir a bow-shot from their standards without being overpowered with an ambush. Let them come on at their pleasure, and when it comes to burning and spoiling you shall see which has the worst of it." "But what will you do with your army if you do not fight," said De Vienne; "and how will your people endure the distress and famine and plunder which must be the consequences of the invasion?" "You shall see that our army shall not be idle," was the reply; "and as for our Scottish people, they will endure pillage, and they will endure famine, and every other extremity of war, but they will not endure English masters."

The wisdom of this course was proved by subsequent results. The English army by the time it reached Edinburgh had got into the most desperate straits owing to the scarcity of provisions. Multitudes perished from want, and to escape total destruction a retreat was ordered through those very districts "which their own merciless and short-sighted policy had rendered a blackened desert."

There is one important fact brought before us in this connection which demands a passing notice. The Reformers have often been severely censured for the wholesale destruction of the ancient Abbeys so intimately associated with the "fair humanities" of the ritual and worship of the Church of Rome. The saying attributed to Knox, about pulling down the rookeries to prevent the crows building, has served as a convenient text for many a philippic on the iconoclastic spirit and tendency of Protestantism. But the truth is that Knox had as little sympathy with what he calls the "rascal multitude," which sometimes engaged in this kind of work, as any of those opposed to him. Our Abbeys for the most part owe their destruction not to Reforming zeal, but to Catholic England's cupidity and revenge. The beautiful Abbeys of Melrose, Dryburgh, and Newbattle were given to the flames by the English soldiers at this time, and the wanton destruction of these noble edifices created in the Scottish mind a feeling of deep and bitter hostility. Jedburgh, too, owes its destruction not to Scottish iconoclasm, but to English invasion. It was pillaged and partly burned by the Earl of Surrey in the year 1523, and its destruction was practically completed by the Earl of Hereford twenty-two years afterwards; so that, so far at least as the Border Abbeys are concerned, the charge so often preferred against the Reformers is a base and stupid calumny.

It was this invasion of the English army which led the Scottish nobles to organise the expedition which may be said to have terminated so gloriously at Otterburn. "The Scots," says Godscroft, "irritated herewith boyled with desire and revenge, being at that time very flourishing with strong youth, and never better furnished with commanders." The barons did not think it politic, for various reasons, to take the King into their confidence. He was of an essentially pacific disposition, and moreover was well stricken in years, and it is almost certain, had the matter been laid before him, he would have opposed the movement to the utmost of his power. His sons, however, were prepared to give every encouragement and assistance, and the barons in order to allay suspicion, and especially to prevent the English getting to know their purposes and plans, assembled at a great feast in Aberdeen and took counsel together. But, as Froissart says, "Everything is known to them who are diligent in their inquiries." The English nobles sent spies to Aberdeen, who, appearing in the guise of heralds and minstrels, became familiar with the plans of the Scottish barons, and speedily carried the information back to their own country. When the Scottish army ultimately assembled at Yetholm, close to the English Border, the English lords were well informed on nearly every point on which information could be desired. Such a muster had not been seen, so it was said, for sixty years. "There were twelve hundred spears, and forty thousand other men and archers. These lords were well pleased on meeting with each other, and declared they would never return to their homes without making an inroad on England, and to such an effect as would be remembered for twenty years."

The English had arranged that, if the Scots entered the country through Cumberland and Carlisle, they would ride into Scotland by Berwick and Dunbar, for they said, theirs is an open country that can be entered anywhere, but ours is a country with strong and well fortified towns and castles. It was therefore important they should know what route the Scots had determined upon. To ascertain this they sent a spy to the Scots' camp that he might report to them not only their intentions, but their speeches and actions. The English squire who came on this errand had a singular and exciting experience. He tied his horse to a tree in the neighbourhood of the church, where the barons were assembled, and entered into the church, as a servant following his master. When he came out he went to get his horse, but to his consternation the animal had disappeared, "for a Scotsman (for they are all thieves) had stolen him.". He went away, saying nothing about his loss, a circumstance which at once excited suspicion. One who saw him remarked, "I have witnessed many wonderful things, but what I now see is equal to any; that man yonder has, I believe, lost his horse, and yet he makes no inquiries after it. On my troth, I doubt much if he belongs to us; let us go after him, and see whether I am right or not." He was immediately apprehended, brought back, and examined. He was told that if he tried to deceive them he would lose his head, but if he told the truth he would be kindly treated. Being in dread of his life, he divulged all he knew, and especially explained with minuteness of detail the plans which had been concocted by his compatriots for the invasion of Scotland. "When the Scottish lords heard what was said they were silent; but looked at each other."

It was now resolved to divide the army into two sections; one section, and that much the larger of the two, to go into England through Cumberland, the other to proceed along the valley of the Tyne to Durham. The latter company, under the command of the Earl of Douglas, made a rapid march through Northumberland, keeping a "calm sough" all the way, but as soon as they got into the neighbourhood of Durham the fiends of war were let loose. The first intimation the garrison in Newcastle had that the enemy was within their gates, was the dense volumes of smoke which ascended from burning towns and homesteads. Having gathered together an immense quantity of booty, the Scots set out on their return journey, and crossing the Tyne assaulted Newcastle, filling the ditches with hay and faggots, hoping thereby to have drawn out the enemy to the open fields. But the English, being in doubt as to the real strength of the Scots' army, were afraid to challenge an encounter. But Sir Henry Percy, better known as *Hotspur*, being desirous to try his valour, offered to fight the Douglas in single combat. "They mounted on two faire steeds, and ran together with sharp ground spears at outrance; in which encounter the Earl Douglas bore Percie out of his saddle. But the English that were by did rescue him so that he could not come at himself, but he snatched away his spear with his guidon or wither; and waving it aloft, and shaking it, he cried aloud that he would carry it into Scotland as his spoil." The account which Froissart gives of this notable encounter differs in some particulars from the foregoing. He says:—"The sons of the Earl of Northumberland, from their great courage, were always the first barriers, when many valiant deeds were done with lances hand to hand. The Earl of Douglas had a long conflict with Sir Henry Percy, and in it, by gallantry of arms, won his pennon, to the great vexation of Sir Henry and the other English." The Earl of Douglas said, "I will carry this token of your prowess with me to Scotland, and place it on the tower of my castle at Dalkeith that it may be seen from far." "By God, Earl of Douglas," replied Sir Henry, "you shall not even carry it out of Northumberland; be assured you shall never have the pennon to brag of." "You must come then," answered Earl Douglas, "this night and seek for it. I will fix your pennon before my tent, and shall see if you venture to take it away." As the balladist has vigorously put it—

He took a long spear in his hand,
Shod with the metal free,
And for to meet the Douglas there,
He rode right furiouslie.

But O how pale his lady look'd,
Frae aff the castle wa',
When down before the Scottish spear
She saw proud Percy fa'.

"Had we twa been upon the green,
And never an eye to see,
I wad hae had you, flesh and fell;

"But gae ye up to Otterbourne,
And wait there dayis three;
And, if I come not ere three dayis end,
A fause knight ca' ye me."

"The Otterbourne's a bonnie burn;
'Tis pleasant there to be;
But there is nought at Otterbourne,
To feed my men and me.

"The deer rins wild on hill and dale,
The birds fly wild from tree to tree;
But there is neither bread nor kail,
To fend my men and me.

"Yet I will stay at Otterbourne,
Where you shall welcome be;
And, if ye come not at three dayis end,
A fause lord I'll ca' thee."

"Thither will I come," proud Percy said,
"By the might of our Ladye!"
"There will I bide thee," said the Douglass,
"My troth I plight to thee."

They lighted high on Otterbourne,
Upon the bent sae brown;
They lighted high on Otterbourne,
And threw their pallions down.

And he that had a bonnie boy,
Sent out his horse to grass;
And he that had not a bonnie boy,
His ain servant he was.

The Earl of Douglas having withdrawn his gallant troops to Otterburn, in the parish of Elsdon, some thirty-two miles from Newcastle, and within easy reach of the Scottish Border, was strongly urged to proceed towards Carlisle, in order to join the main body of the army; but he thought it best to stay there some three or four days at least, to "repell the Percy's bragging." To keep his soldiers from wearying, he set them to take some gentlemen's castles and houses that lay near, a work which was carried out with the greatest alacrity and goodwill. They also strengthened and fortified the camp where it was weak, and built huts of trees and branches. Their baggage and servants they placed at the entrance of a marsh, which lay near the Newcastle road; and driving their cattle into the marsh land, where they were comparatively safe, they waited the development of events.

Nor were they long kept in suspense. The English having discovered that the Scottish army was comparatively small, resolved at once to risk an encounter. Sir Henry Percy, when he heard that the Scottish army did not consist of more than three thousand men, including all sorts, became frantically excited, and cried out—"To horse! to horse! for by the faith I owe to my God, and to my lord and father, I will seek to recover my pennon, and to beat up their quarters this night." He set out at once, accompanied by six hundred spears, of knights and squires, and upwards of eight thousand infantry, which he said would be more than enough to fight the Scots.

If Providence is always on the side of the heaviest battalion, as Napoleon was wont to affirm, then the Scots on this occasion are in imminent danger of having "short shrift." But it has been found that the fortunes of war depend on a variety of circumstances that are frequently of more importance than the number of troops, either on the one side or the other. Discipline and valour, when combined with patriotism and pride-of-arms, have accomplished feats which the heaviest battalions are sometimes impotent to achieve. We by no means wish to imply that the English were deficient in these desirable qualities; far from it. They were splendidly led, and in the encounter displayed the most heroic qualities; but they were matched by a small body of men, of the most dauntless courage and invincible determination who were thoroughly inured to battle, and ever ready at the call of duty, to encounter the most powerful foes. The Scots were taken by surprise. Some were at supper, and others had gone to rest when the alarm was given that the English were approaching.

But up then spake a little page,
Before the peep of dawn—
"O waken ye, waken ye, my good lord,
For Percy's hard at hand."

"Ye lie, ye lie, ye liar loud!
Sae loud I hear ye lie;
For Percy had not men yestreen,
To dight my men and me.

"But I have dream'd a dreary dream,
Beyond the Isle of Sky;
I saw a dead man win a fight,
And I think that man was I."

He belted on his guid braid sword,
And to the field he ran;
But he forgot the helmit good,
That should have kept his brain.

The battle now raged in earnest. A bright warm day had been followed by a clear still moonlight night. "The fight," says Godscroft, "was continued very hard as among noble men on both sides, who did esteem more of glory than life. Percy strove to repair the foil he got at Newcastle, and the Earl Douglas did as much labour to keep the honour he had won. So in unequal numbers, but both eager in mind, they continued fighting a great part of the night. At last a cloud covering the face of the moon, not being able to discern friend from foe, they took some respite for a while; but so soon as the cloud was gone, the English gave so hard a charge, that the Scots were put back in such sort, that the Douglas standard was in great peril to have been lost. This did so irritate him, that he himself in the one wing, and the two Hepburns (father and son) in the other, pressing through the ranks of their own men, and advancing to the place where the greatest peril appeared, renewed a hard conflict, and by giving and receiving many wounds, they restored their men into the place from whence they had been beaten, and continued the fight till the next day at noon.". Foremost, in the thick of the fray, was the dauntless Douglas, laying about him on every side with a mace of iron, which two ordinary men were not able to lift, "and making a lane round about wheresoever he went."

When Percy wi' the Douglas met
I wat he was fu' fain!
They swakked their swords till sair they swat,
And the blood ran down like rain.

"Thus he advanced like another Hector, thinking to recover and conquer the field, from his own prowess, until he was met by three spears that were pointed at him: one struck him on the shoulder, another on the stomach, near the belly, and the third entered his thigh. He could never disengage himself from these spears, but was borne to the ground fighting desperately. From that moment he never rose again. Some of his knights and squires had followed him, but not all; for though the moon shone it was rather dark. The three English lances knew they had struck down some person of considerable rank, but never thought it was Earl Douglas: had they known it they would have been so rejoiced that their courage would have been redoubled, and the fortune of the day had consequently been determined to their side. The Scots were ignorant also of their loss till the battle was over, otherwise they would certainly, from despair, have been discomfited."

When at last the dying Douglas was discovered by his kinsman, James Lindsay and John and Walter Sinclair, and was asked how he fared, he replied, "I do well dying as my

13

predecessors have done before; not on a bed of lingering sickness, but in the field. These things I require you as my last petitions; First, that ye keep my death close both from my own folk, and from the enemy; then that ye suffer not my standard to be lost, or cast down; and last that ye avenge my death, and bury me at Melrose with my father. If I could hope for these things, I should die with the greater contentment, for long since I heard a prophecy that a dead man should win a field, and I hope in God it shall be I."

"My wound is deep; I fain would sleep,
Take thou the vanguard of the three,
And hide me by the bracken bush,
That grows on yonder lilye lee.

"O bury me by the bracken bush,
Beneath the blooming brier,
Let never living mortal ken,
A kindly Scot lies here."

Throwing a shroud over the prostrate body of the wounded and dying soldier, that the enemy might not discover who it was that had fallen, they raised the standard and shouted lustily "a Douglas! a Douglas!" and rushed with might and main upon the English host. Soon the English ranks began to waver, and when at last it was known that Hotspur had been taken prisoner by the Earl of Montgomery, "The enemy fled and turned their backs." According to Godscroft there were 1840 of the English slain, 1040 taken prisoners, and 1000 wounded. The losses on the Scottish, according to the same historian, were comparatively trifling, amounting only to 100 slain and 200 taken prisoners.

This deed was done at Otterbourne
About the breaking of the day,
Earl Douglas was buried at the bracken bush,
And the Percy led captive away.

There are several incidents connected with this famous battle that are worthy of special notice, but one in particular demands a passing word. The Bishop of Durham, at the head of ten thousand men, appeared on the field almost immediately after the battle had ended. The Scots were greatly alarmed, and scarcely knew how, in the circumstances,—having so many prisoners and wounded to attend to,—they were to meet this formidable host. They fortified their camp, having only one pass by which it could be entered; made their prisoners swear that, whether rescued or not, they would remain their prisoners; and then they ordered their minstrels to play as merrily as possible. The Bishop of Durham had scarcely approached within a league of the Scots when they began to play such a concert that "it seemed as if all the devils in hell had come thither to join in the noise," so that those of the English who had never before heard such were much frightened. As he drew nearer, the noise became more terrific—"the hills redoubling the sound." The Bishop being impressed with the apparent strength of the camp, and not a little alarmed at the discordant piercing sounds which proceeded from it, thought it desirable to retreat as speedily as possible, as it appeared to him that there were greater chances of loss than gain. "He was affrighted with the sound of the horns."

Thus ended one of the most notable battles on record. The flower of the chivalry of both nations took part in it, and never did men acquit themselves with greater credit. Indeed it is generally admitted that the valour displayed on both sides has rarely, if ever, been surpassed. But perhaps most notable of all was the kindness and consideration displayed towards those who had been wounded or taken prisoner. The former were tended with the greatest care; and as for the latter, the most of them were permitted to go back to their homes, after having given their word of honour that they would return when called upon. Not more than four hundred prisoners were carried into Scotland, and some of these were allowed to regain their liberty by naming their own ransom.

Many severe accusations have been brought against Scotsmen, and especially Borderers, for their cruelty and inhumanity in time of war. It is perhaps possible to make good this indictment; but we do not believe that in regard to such matters the Scots were worse than their neighbours. And if they had great vices, they had also splendid virtues. They were brave, truthful, courteous, too ready perhaps to draw the sword on the slightest provocation, but as has been shown in the present instance, they were incapable of taking a mean advantage of a fallen foe. They loved fighting for its own sake, as well as for the sake of the "booty," but when the battle was over they cherished few resentments. The splendid qualities, physical and moral, so conspicuously brought to view in the battle of Otterburn cannot fail to suggest what a magnificent country Scotland might have become many centuries ago had she only been blessed with wise Kings and a strong Government.

III.

POOR AND LAWLESS.

"Mountainous and strange is the country,
And the people rough and savage."

e have seen that the feeling of hatred to the English which prevailed on the Scottish Borders was due to some extent to the memory of the wrongs which the Borderers had suffered at the hands of their hereditary enemies. That this feeling had something to do with the existence and development of the reiving system, must be apparent to every student of history and of human nature. It was the most natural thing in the world that the dwellers on the Scottish Border should seek to retaliate; and as the forces at their command were seldom powerful enough to justify their engaging in open warfare, they resorted to the only other method of revenge which held out to them any hope of success.

But while this aspect of the situation ought to be kept prominently in view, there are other factors of the problem which must not be overlooked. In the Middle Ages the district of country known as the Borders must have presented a very different appearance from what it does at the close of the 19th century. The Merse, which is now, for the most part, in a high state of cultivation, and capable of bearing the finest crops, was then in a comparatively poor condition, looked at from an agricultural point of view. The soil in many places was thin, poor, and marshy. Drainage was unknown, and the benefits accruing from the rotation of crops, and the system of feeding the soil with artificial manures, so familiar in these days of high farming, were then very inadequately appreciated. Perhaps an exception to this statement ought to be made in favour of the land held and cultivated by the great religious houses, such as Melrose, Jedburgh, and Kelso. The tenants on these lands enjoyed special privileges and immunities, and were thus able to prosecute their labour not only with more skill, but with a greater certainty of success. It is sometimes said that the monks knew where to pitch their camps; that they appropriated to their own use and benefit the fairest and richest parts of the country; but,

15

as Lord Hailes very pertinently remarks, "When we examine the sites of ancient Monasteries, we are sometimes inclined to say with the vulgar, that the clergy in former times always chose the best of the land, and the most commodious habitations, but we do not advert, that religious houses were frequently erected on waste grounds, afterwards improved by the art and industry of the clergy, who alone had art and industry." The land held by these houses was cultivated on more or less scientific principles. "Within the precincts of the wealthier abbeys," says Skelton, "an active industrial community was housed. The prescribed offices of the church were of course scrupulously observed: but the energies of the society were not exclusively occupied with, nor indeed mainly directed to, the performance of religious duties. The occupants of the monasteries wore the religious garb; but they were road-makers, farmers, merchants, lawyers, as well as priests.... The earliest roads in Scotland that deserved the name were made by the Monks and their dependents; and were intended to connect the religious houses as trading societies with the capital or nearest seaport. A decent public road is indispensable to an industrial community: and a considerable portion of the trade of the country was in the hands of the religious orders. The Monks of Melrose sent wool to the Netherlands; others trafficked in corn, in timber, in salmon.... Each community, each order, as was natural, had its characteristic likings and dislikings. One house turned out the best scholars and lawyers, another the finest wool and the sweetest mutton; one was famed for poetry and history, another for divinity or medicine.". It would therefore be nearer the truth to say that the monks made the districts in which they lived rich and fertile; than that they found them so, and took possession of them in consequence.

But beyond the sphere of these monastic institutions, the state of matters from an agricultural point of view could hardly have been worse. This was mainly due to the fact that, so far as Berwickshire and some parts of Dumfriesshire are concerned, the tiller of the soil was never sure that he would have the privilege of reaping his harvest. By the time the grain was ready for the sickle an English army might invade the country and give the crops to the flames. This happened so frequently, and the feeling of insecurity thus became so great, that husbandry at times was all but abandoned. There can be no doubt that this was one prime factor in creating the poverty which was so long a marked and painful feature of the life of the Scottish Borders.

On the other hand, there was a considerable extent of country, extending from Jedburgh to Canobie, which was practically unfit for cultivation. The Royal Forest of Ettrick was of great extent, and was reserved as a happy hunting ground for the Court and its minions. Along the banks of the Teviot and the Liddle, embracing a considerable portion of Roxburgh and Dumfries, the extent of land capable of cultivation was by no means great, even though it had been found practical, or politic, to put it under the ploughshare. This region is one of the most mountainous in the South of Scotland, and in ancient times abounded in quaking bogs and inaccessible morasses. This district naturally became the favourite haunt of the Border reiver. Here he could find ways and means either of securing his own cattle, or those he had "lifted," from the search of the enemy by driving them into some inaccessible retreat, the entrance to which it was difficult, if not impossible, for strangers to discover.

Of the general condition of the country at this time a vivid picture has been given by Æneas Sylvius, one of the Piccolomini, afterwards Pius II., who visited Scotland in the year 1413. He thus writes:—"Concerning Scotland he found these things worthy of repetition. It is an *island joined* to England, stretching two hundred miles to the North, and about fifty broad: a cold country, fertile of few sorts of grain, and generally void of trees, but there is a sulphureous stone dug up which is used for firing. The towns are unwalled, the houses commonly built without lime, and in villages roofed with turf, while a cow's hide supplies the place of a door. The commonalty are poor and uneducated, have abundance of flesh and fish, but eat bread as a dainty. The men are small in stature, but bold; the women fair and comely, and prone to the pleasures of love, kisses being esteemed of less consequence than pressing the hand is in Italy. The wine is all imported; the horses are mostly small ambling nags, only a few being preserved entire for propagation; and neither curry-combs nor reins are used. From Scotland are imported into Flanders hides, wool, salt, fish, and pearls. *Nothing gives the Scots more pleasure than to hear the English dispraised.* The country is divided into two parts, the cultivated lowlands, and the region where agriculture is not used. The wild Scots have a different language, and sometimes eat the bark of trees. There are no wolves. Crows are new inhabitants, and therefore the tree in which they build becomes royal property. At the winter, when the author was there, the day did not exceed four hours."

That there are several inaccuracies in this account goes without saying, but they are just such mistakes as a person making a hurried run through the country would very naturally commit. Wolves and crows were much more plentiful at that period than the inhabitants wished, as may be seen from various Acts of Parliament which were passed in order to promote their destruction. But the general description of the country here given agrees, in its main details, with other contemporary records, and presents a truly dismal picture of the poverty of the people.

Even as late as the 16th century there were few well-formed roads, other than those already mentioned. There were no posts, either for letters or for travelling. Education was confined to the library of the Convent, where the sons of the barons were taught dialectic and grammar. Society consisted mainly of the agricultural class, who were half enslaved to the lords of the soil, and obliged to follow them in war. The people were fearfully rude and ignorant, much more so than the English—in this respect, indeed, contrasting unfavourably with almost any other European State. Few of them could either read or write; even the most powerful barons were often unable to sign their names. As might be expected in such a condition of society, the nobles exercised great oppression on the poor. The Government of the country was a mere faction of the nobility as against all the rest. It is said that when a man had a suit at law he felt he had no chance without using "influence." Was he to be tried for an offence, his friends considered themselves bound to muster in arms around the court to see that he got justice; that is, to get him off unpunished if they could. Men were accustomed to violence in all forms as to their daily bread. "The hail realm of Scotland was sae divided in factions that it was hard to get any peaceable man as he rode out the hie way, to profess himself openly, either to be a favourer to the King or Queen. All the people were castin sae lowss, and were become of sic dissolute minds and actions, that nane was in account but he that could either kill or reive his neighbours.".

Such facts as these indicate in a remarkable way the extraordinary weakness of the executive government. It is abundantly evident that the Scottish Parliament was most exemplary in passing measures for the protection and amelioration of the people, but as Buchanan naively remarks, "There was ane Act of Parliament needed in Scotland, a decree to enforce the observance of the others." The King's writ did not run in many districts of the country. The unfortunate element in the situation was that it did not always coincide with the interests of the nobles to see that the decrees of the Estates were carried into effect; and as a general rule what did not happen to accord with their humour was set aside as of no moment. The consequence was that many Acts of Parliament, relating especially to the abnormal condition of the Borders, were no sooner passed than they were treated as practically obsolete. This accounts for the curious fact that we find the legislature returning again and again, at brief intervals, to the consideration of the same questions, and issuing orders which might as well never have been recorded. When the counsels of a nation are thus divided, and especially when those who are charged with the administration of the law pay no regard to it, in their own persons, it would be a marvel if lawlessness in its multifarious forms did not become the dominant characteristic of the great body of the people. That this was the result produced is painfully evident. The great barons were practically supreme within their own domains, for while the execution of the laws might nominally pertain to the Sovereign, the soldiers belonged to their Chiefs, and were absolutely at their command. Laws which cannot be enforced at the point of the sword must in the nature of the case remain practically inoperative. This unfortunate condition of affairs was a fruitful source of misery and mischief, especially on the Borders, where the prevalence of the clan-system conferred on the Chiefs the most arbitrary and far-reaching powers. Had there been any possibility of bringing the Border barons under effective governmental control "the thefts, herschips, and slaughters," for which this district was so long notorious, would have been in great part prevented. These men not only incited to crime, but standing as they did between the ruler and the ruled, they threw the ægis of their protection over the lawless and disobedient.

If only that nation is to be reckoned happy which has few laws, but is accustomed to obey them, then Scotland, and the Borders in particular, must have been in a most unfortunate condition during a lengthened period of its history. The laws passed were numerous; the obedience rendered most difficult to discover. But while these enactments rarely succeeded in producing the results aimed at, they are, notwithstanding, exceedingly valuable to the historian because of the interesting light they cast on the conditions and habits of the people. In the year 1567, in the first Parliament of James VI., an important Act was passed, entitled "Anent Theft and Receipt of Theft, Taking of Prisoners by Thieves, or Bands for Ransoms, and Punishment of the same." It relates especially to the Sheriffdoms of Selkirk, Roxburgh, Peebles, Dumfries, and Edinburgh, "and other inhabitants of the remanent Shires of the Realm," bearing that it is not unknown of the continual theft, reif, and oppression committed within the bounds of the said Sheriffdoms, by thieves, traitors, and other ungodly persons, having neither fear of God nor man, which is the chief cause of the said thefts. And that the said thieves and "broken men" commit daily "thefts, reifs, herschips, murders, and fire raisings" upon the peaceable subjects of the country, "besides also takes sundrie of them," detains them in captivity as prisoners, ransoms them, "or lettis them to borrowis for their entrie again." In like manner, it is said, divers subjects of the inland, take and sit under their assurance paying them blackmail, and permitting them to "reif, herrie, and oppress their nichtbouris" with their knowledge and in their sight, without resistance or contradiction.

To remove these inconveniences it was statute and ordained that whoever receipted, fortified, maintained, or gave meat, harbourage, or assistance to any thieves in their theftuous stealing or deeds, either coming thereto, or passing therefrom, or intercommunes or trysts with them, without licence of the keeper of the country, where the thief remains shall be called therefore at particular diets "criminally other airt and pairt in their theftuous deeds," or proceeded against civilly, after fifteen days warning, "without diet or tabill." It was further ordained under pain of lese majesty, that no true and faithful lieges taken by these men should be holden to enter to them, all bonds to the contrary notwithstanding. And if anyone should happen to take and apprehend any of the said thieves, either in passing to commit said theft, or in the actual doing thereof, or in their returning thencefrom, he was in no case to set them at liberty; but to present them before the Justice, and his deputies in the tolbooth of Edinburgh, within fifteen days, "gif their takeris justifye them not to the death them selfis." Further, it was ordained that none take assurance, or sit under assurance of said thieves, or pay them blackmail, or give them meat or drink, under pain of death. In like manner when thieves repaired to steal or reive within the incountry the lieges were commanded to rise, cry, and raise the fray and follow them, coming or going, on horse and foot, for recovery of the goods stolen, and apprehending of their persons, under pain of being held partakers in the said theft. It was also added that if any open and notorious thief came to a house, the owner of the house might apprehend him without reproach.

These enactments are at once minute and comprehensive, and had the power to enforce them corresponded in any degree with the good intentions of those who framed them, there would have been a considerable change produced in the affairs of the Border. But the truth is these so-called statutes were but little better than mere "pious opinions," reflecting credit on those responsible for them, but producing no impression, or next to none, on the country. Not many years after the passing of these Acts we find the Estates busy at work again passing measure after measure for the quieting of the disordered subjects on the Borders, for the staunching of theft and slaughter, and the punishment of "wicked thieves and limmers." Things had gone from bad to worse. Every man's hand was against his neighbour. Clan rose against clan; the Scotts and the Kerrs, the Maxwells and Johnstones, were constantly embroiled in petty warfare, the results of which, however, were sometimes most disastrous. "The broken men"—Græmes, Armstrongs, Bells, and other inhabitants of the Debateable land—finding it either unsafe or inconvenient to commit such frequent "herschips" on the English border, betook themselves with all their accustomed enthusiasm to the plundering of their Scottish neighbours. They are described as "delighting in all mischief, and maist unnaturally and cruelly wasting and destroying, harrying and slaying, their own neighbours." The Privy Council at last determined to deal with these matters, and arranged to sit on the first day of every month in the year for this purpose. Trial and injunction was to be taken of the diligence done in the execution of things directed the month preceding, and of things necessary and expedient to be put in execution during the next month to come, and that a special register be kept of all that shall happen to be done and directed in matters concerning the quietness and good rule of the Borders. But to make assurance doubly sure it was also ordained at the same time that all landlords and bailies of the lands, should find sufficient caution and surety, under pain of rebellion, to bring all persons guilty of "reife, theft, receipt of theft, depredations, open and avowed fire-raisings, upon deadly feud, protected and maintained by their masters," before "our sovereign lord's Justice," to underlie the law for the same. Failing their doing so, the landlords and bailies were bound to satisfy the party skaithed, and to refund, content, and pay to them their "herschips and skaithes." And further, the chief of the clan, in the bounds where "broken men" dwell, and to which "broken men" repair in their passing to steal and reive, or returning therefrom, shall be bound to make the like stay and arrestment, and publication as the landlords or bailies, and be subject to the like redress, criminal and civil, in case of their failure and negligence. In addition to the foregoing ordinances, it was resolved that all Captains, Chiefs, and Chieftains of the clans, dwelling on the lands of divers landlords, shall enter pledges for those over whom they exercise authority, upon fifteen days' notice, before his Highness and his secret Council, said pledges to be placed as his Highness shall deem convenient—"for the good rule in time coming, according to the conditions above written whereunto the landlords and bailies are subject; under the pain of the execution of the said pledges to the death, and no redress made by the persons offended for whom the pledges lie."

We also learn from another Act of Parliament, passed at the same time, that all pledges received for the good rule and quietness of the Border shall be placed on the north side of the water of Forth, without exception or dispensation; and the pledges for the good rule of the Highlands and Isles, to be placed on the south side of the same water of Forth.

But one of the most extraordinary Acts passed by this Parliament was an Act forbidding the Scottish Borderers to marry the daughters of the "broken men" or thieves of England, as it was declared this was "not only a hindrance to his Majesty's service and obedience, but also to the common peace and quietness betwixt both the Realms." It was therefore statute and ordained "that nane of the subjects presume to take upon hand to marrie with onie English woman, dwelling in the opposite Marches, without his Highness' express licence, had and obtained to that effect, under the great Seal; under the paine of death, and confiscation of all his goods moveable; and this be a special point of dittay in time cumming."

These enactments were doubtless well meant, and under ordinary circumstances might have been expected to bring about beneficial results; but unfortunately they were treated with callous indifference. No improvement was effected. The "broken men" were not to be intimidated by such measures. They laughed at Parliament, and scorned the laws. This is brought out in the most conclusive manner in the records of the State Paper Office, as we shall have occasion to point out in succeeding chapters. But proof of another kind lies ready to hand. An Act of Parliament was passed in 1593, just six years after those already noticed, in which complaint is made of the rebellious contempt of his Highness' subjects who, without regard of their dutiful obedience, pass daily to the horn, "for not finding of law surety;" and "for not subscribing of assurances in matter of feud," and for "dinging and stricking his Majesty's messengers," in execution of their offices. Notice is also taken of some who nightly and daily reive, foray, and commit open theft and oppression: "for remead whereof, our said Sovereign Lord, ordains the Acts and laws made before to be put to execution, and ratifies and approves the same in all points." It was further ordained that no respite or remission was to be granted at any time hereafter to any person or persons that pass to the horn for "theft, reif, slauchter, burning or heir-shippe, while the party skaithed be first satisfied; and gif ony respite or remission shall happen to be granted, before the partie grieved be first satisfied, the samin shall be null and of nane avail, be way of exception or reply, without any further declaritour; except the saidis remissiones and respittes be granted, for pacifying of the broken Countries and Borders."

These may be regarded as fair samples of the long list of measures passed at different times by the Scottish Parliament for the regulation of Border affairs during the reign of the Jameses. In reading them one is forcibly reminded of a remark made by one of the English wardens, that "things were very tickle on the Scottish Border." No respect was paid to the law, either by the Chiefs or their clansmen. In the preface to Cary's Memoirs, these Scottish Borderers are described as "equalling the Caffirs in the trade of stealing, and the Hottentots in ignorance and brutality." This savage indictment is borne out by Sir William Bowes who, in a letter to Burghley in the year 1593—nearly forty years after the Reformation—thus writes:—"The opposite wardens and officers being always Borderers bred and dwelling there, also cherish favourites and strengthen themselves by the worst disposed, to support their factions. And as they are often changed by the King for their misdemeanours, the new man always refuses to answer for attempts before his time. Cessford the warden cannot answer for the whole Middle March, but must seek to Fernihirst for one part, and Buccleuch for Teviotdale.

"*Execrable murders are constantly committed*, whereof 4 new complaints were made to the lords in the few days they were here, and 3 others this month in Atholstonmoor. The gentlemen of the Middle March recount out of their memories nearly 200 Englishmen, miserably murdered by the Scots, since the tenth year of her Majesty's reign, for which no redress hath at all been made.... I have presumed to testify this much to your lordship more tediously than I should; yet will be ready to do more particularly, if you direct me. Praying you to receive from some other, equally heedful of truth—and in meantime trusting you will cover my name from undeserved offence—I pray God to make you an instrument under our gracious sovereign to cure the aforesaid gangrene thus noisomely molesting the foot of this kingdom."

This "gangrene" was of long standing, and as we shall find was not to be easily eradicated.

But while poverty,—largely due to circumstances over which the people had no control,—and lawlessness,—the result of the inherent weakness of the central government,—had much to do in creating that condition of affairs on the Borders which we have briefly described, there were other and perhaps more potent causes which demand consideration. Foremost among these was the almost entire absence of the restraints and sanctions of religion. In one of the Acts of Parliament already noticed it is significantly declared that one of the principal causes of the lawlessness of the Borders was that "they had neither the fear of God nor man." To those familiar with certain phases of Border history this may appear somewhat anomalous. At an early period in the religious life of Scotland this district was brought under the influence of the Evangel by St. Aidan and St. Cuthbert. That the work of these missionaries was signally successful, is shown in the large number of churches planted all over the Borderland. After the time of Queen Margaret, whose influence in certain directions was almost marvellously potent, the great religious houses of the Borders rose in rapid succession, such as Melrose, Kelso, and Jedburgh, each a centre and source of religious and social wellbeing. The moral life of the people, notwithstanding the existence of such beneficent institutions, may have been of an indifferent character; but what the state of matters might have been, had those places, and what they represented, never been in existence at all, it is impossible to conceive. It was a true instinct which led the people to regard the Abbey of Haddington as the "Lamp of the Lothians." And the same designation might have been applied with equal appropriateness to every Abbey in the country. Those places for many generations represented all that was highest and best in the thought and life of Mediævalism. Here law and order were supreme. Round those religious houses industrial, orderly communities sprang up, whose influence was felt throughout the length and breadth of the land. The Monasteries may deserve all that was said of them in later times, but, throughout a considerable period of their history, their influence was almost wholly beneficial. Scotland owes much to them, and there is no reason why the fact should not be generously recognised. It is no doubt true that, for some considerable time before the Reformation, those great institutions had sadly degenerated. "Jeshurun waxed fat and kicked." The time came when they had, perforce, to yield to those disintegrating processes which usually herald the advent of reform. The old order changeth. The new wine of a democratic Protestantism, in which the claims of the individual, his right to think for himself, and form his own judgments, are prominent ingredients, agreed but indifferently with the old bottles of an earlier Faith and Polity. And so the Monasteries disappeared.

But it was long ere the new light of the Reformation made itself practically felt on the Borders. When the influences which had hitherto been so potent ceased to operate, a condition of religious and moral chaos supervened. Hundreds of churches were left without ministers. Whole districts practically lapsed into barbarism. For at least fifty years after the Reformation, the Scottish Borders were to all intents and purposes out-with the influence of the Church. Even as late as the Covenanting period their condition had not greatly improved. "We learn," says Sir Walter Scott, "from a curious passage in the life of Richard Cameron, a fanatical preacher during what is called the time of 'persecution,' that some of the Borderers retained till a late period their indifference about religious matters. After having been licensed at Haughead, in Teviotdale, he was, according to his biographer, sent first to preach in Annandale. 'He said, How can I go there? I know what sort of people they are.' But Mr Welch said, 'Go your way, Ritchie, and set the fire of hell to their tails.' He went, and the first day he preached on the text— *How shall I put thee among the children, &c.* In the application he said, 'Put you among the children! the offspring of thieves and robbers! we have all heard of Annandale thieves.' Some of them got a merciful cast that day, and told afterwards that it was the first field meeting they had ever attended, and that they went out of mere curiosity, to see a minister preach in a tent, and people sit on the ground."

During the period of religious decadence, prior to the Reformation, a remarkable custom, not unknown elsewhere, prevailed on the Borders. Owing to the scarcity of clergymen, especially in the Vales of Ewes, Esk, and Liddle, the rites of the church were only intermittently celebrated, a circumstance which gave rise to what was known as *Hand-fasting*. Loving couples who met at fairs and other places of public resort agreed to live together for a certain period, and if, when the *book-a-bosom* man, as the itinerant clergyman was called, came to pay his yearly visit to the district, they were still disposed to remain in wedlock they received the blessing of the church; but if it should happen that either party was dissatisfied, then the union might be terminated, on the express condition, however, that the one desiring to withdraw should become responsible for the maintenance of the child, or children, which may have been born to them. "The connection so formed was binding for one year only, at the expiration of which time either party was at liberty to withdraw from the engagement, or in the event of both being satisfied the 'hand-fasting' was renewed for life. The custom is mentioned by several authors, and was by no means confined to the lower classes, John Lord Maxwell and a sister of the Earl of Angus being thus contracted in January 1577."

IV.

RAIDS AND FORAYS.

"Then forward bound both horse and hound,
And rattle o'er the vale;
As the wintry breeze through leafless trees
Drives on the pattering hail.

"Behind their course the English fells
In deepening blue retire;
Till soon before them boldly swells
The muir of dun Redswire."

    Leyden.

To give anything like an adequate account of the various raids and forays, on the one side of the Border and the other, would fill many volumes. These raids, as we have already noticed, began at an early period, and were carried on almost without intermission for at least three hundred years. The Armstrongs and Elliots in Liddesdale, and many of the other noted clans in Merse and Teviotdale, were "always riding." As an English warden remarks in one of his despatches to the Government:—"They lie still never a night"—a statement which may be accepted as literally true. At some point or other along the Border line, invasions either on the part of the Scots or English were constantly occurring. In this respect, more especially during the reign of Queen Elizabeth, the Scots were perhaps the principal offenders. But as a general rule their invasions, though frequent, were on a comparatively small scale, partaking rather of the nature of forays than of raids. They would hurriedly cross the Border of an evening, drive together as many cattle or sheep as they could find, and then hasten back with all possible speed to their own country. Sometimes, if they were compelled to go a considerable distance inland, they would hide during the day in some quiet glen, within the enemy's territory, and then sally forth as soon as the moon lent her kindly aid, and accomplish with the utmost expedition the task which had brought them thither. It is said that these incursions were marked with the desire of spoil rather than of slaughter, a statement which may be true so far as forays generally are concerned, but which certainly does not apply to the more important raids. These latter incursions were marked with every element of ferocity and bloodshed. In some of the raids conducted by Cessford and Buccleuch, in the 15th century, in Redesdale and Tynedale, many lives were sacrificed, and all who offered resistance were put to the sword. Hertford, Wharton, and others, in their raids upon the Scottish Border seemed often more intent on shedding blood than securing booty. The statement that these incursions were marked with a desire of spoil rather than bloodshed must therefore be accepted *cum grano salis.*

It would seem that the season of year most favourable to reiving was between Michaelmas and Martinmas. The reason of this is not difficult to discover. The reivers in their expeditions hardly ever went on foot. They rode small hackneys—hardy, well-built animals—on which they cantered over hill and dale, moor and meadow, a circumstance which gained for them the name of *hobylers.* In the late autumn the moors and mosses were drier than at any other season of the year, which made riding, in certain districts especially, a much more easy and expeditious undertaking. Then the winter supply had to be secured. The beef tub required replenishing, and as the "mart" was rarely ever fed at home it had to be sought for elsewhere. It was a case of all hands to work, and every available horse or rider was brought into requisition.

Leslie has given a graphic description of the methods adopted by the Border reivers to secure their booty. Everything was gone about in the most orderly and deliberate manner. He says that the reivers never told their beads with so much devotion as when they were setting out on a marauding expedition, and expected a good booty as a recompense of their devotion! "They sally out of their own borders in troops, through unfrequented ways and many intricate windings. In the day time they refresh themselves and their horses in lurking places they had pitched on before, till they arrive in the dark at those places they have a design upon. As soon as they have seized upon their booty, they, in like manner, return home in the night; through blind ways and fetching many a compass. The more skilful any captain is to pass through these wild deserts, crooked turnings, and deep precipices, in the thickest mists and darkness, his reputation is the greater, and he is looked upon as a man of an excellent head, and they are so very cunning, that they seldom have their booty taken from them, unless sometimes, when by the help of bloodhounds, following them exactly upon the track, they may chance to fall into the hands of their adversaries. When being taken they have so much persuasive eloquence, and so many smooth and insinuating words at command, that if they do not move their judges, nay and even their adversaries, to have mercy, yet they incite them to admiration and compassion."

Such a skilful "Captain," as is here referred to, was the famous Hobbie Noble, who terminated his adventurous career in "Merrie Carlisle," where so many famous freebooters, at one time or other, have paid the last penalty of the law. Speaking of himself, he says:—

"But will ye stay till the day gae down,
Until the night come o'er the ground,
And I'll be a guide worth ony twa
That may in Liddisdale be found!

"Though the night be dark as pick and tar,
I'll guide ye o'er yon hill sae hie;
And bring ye a' in safety back,
If ye'll be true and follow me."

But the skill of the leader of the foray was not always sufficient to bring his followers safely back to their homes and families. When the bloodhounds were put on the track it was often a matter of the greatest difficulty for the thieves to elude their pursuers.

"The russet bloodhound wont, near Annand's stream,
To trace the sly thief with avenging foot
Close as an evil conscience."

These useful animals were kept at different points along the Border, and as they rendered most important services, we are not surprised to learn that a good sleuth-hound often sold as high as a hundred crowns.

It may be interesting, before proceeding to give an account of some of the more famous raids, to glance briefly at the manner in which the raiders were armed and accoutred for the fray. Froissart has given the following account of the Scottish Borderers, and Scottish soldiers generally, as they appeared towards the close of the fourteenth century. "The Scots," he says, "are bold, hardy, and much inured to war. When they make their invasions into England, they march from twenty to four-and-twenty leagues without halting, as well by night as by day; for they are all on horseback, except the camp followers, who are on foot. The knights and esquires are mounted on large bay horses, the common people on little Galloways. They bring no carriages with them, on account of the mountains they have to pass in Northumberland; neither do they carry with them any provisions of bread and wine, for the habits of sobriety are such in time of war that they will live a long time on flesh half sodden, without bread, and drink the river water without wine. They have therefore no occasion for pots or pans, for they dress the flesh of their cattle in the skins after they have taken them off; and being sure to find plenty of them in the country which they invade, they carry none with them. Under the flaps of his saddle each man carries a broad plate of metal, behind the saddle a little bag of oatmeal. When they have eaten too much of the sodden flesh, and their stomach appears weak and empty, they place this plate over the fire, mix with water their oatmeal, and when the plate is heated they put a little of the paste upon it and make a thin cake like a cracknel or biscuit, which they eat to warm their stomachs; it is therefore no wonder they perform a longer day's march than other soldiers. In this manner the Scots entered England, destroying and burning everything as they passed. They seized more cattle than they knew what to do with. Their army consisted of four thousand men at arms, knights, and esquires, well mounted, besides twenty thousand men, bold and hardy, armed after the manner of their country, and mounted upon little hackneys that are never tied up or dressed, but are turned immediately after the day's march to pasture on the heath or in the field."

It may be said that this description—which, it may be remarked, is as graphic in outline as it is minute in detail—applies rather to the regular army than to those undisciplined marauding bands which infested the Borders, and to which the name "reivers" or "mosstroopers" is usually assigned. This is no doubt true. At the same time, it must not be forgotten that many of the more important raids were undertaken by large bodies of troops, numbering sometimes three or four thousand men. This much at least is certain that the Border reiver was always well mounted, and well armed with lance or spear, which, on occasion, he could use with much dexterity and skill. With a steel cap on his head, a jack slung over his shoulders, a pistol or hagbut at his belt, he was ever ready for the fray, and prepared to give or take the hardest blows. He was naturally fond of fighting. Like Dandie Dinmont's terriers he never could get enough of it, and must have found life peculiarly irksome when he was compelled to desist from his favourite pastime. He lived in the saddle, and was as unaccustomed to the ordinary occupations of the world as the wild Arab of the desert.

Even to enumerate the raids and forays on the one side or the other, of which some record has been left either in the Histories of the two Kingdoms, or in the archives of the State Paper Office, would be an almost endless task, and moreover would serve no really useful purpose. The details of the "burnings," "herschips," and "slaughters," which were the necessary concomitants of these invasions, are much the same in all cases. It is a dreary tale of theft and oppression, bloodshed and murder. The following incidents may be taken as fairly illustrative examples.

During the reign of Henry VIII. the relations between the two kingdoms were often of a most unsatisfactory and unsettled character. This was due to a variety of causes, partly political and partly religious. The same difficulties cropped up in the subsequent reigns of Edward, Mary, and Elizabeth, and the consequence was that war clouds were ever hanging, dark and threatening, on the horizon. The mutual antagonism between the two countries fostered the raiding tendencies of both kingdoms. The Scots were intent on despoiling their more wealthy neighbours, and the English never missed an opportunity of humiliating and crippling their ancient foes.

Two of the most destructive invasions, or raids, on the part of the English were conducted by the Earl of Hertford and Sir Ralph Eure. The former invaded the country both by sea and land. Edinburgh and Leith suffered severely. The Abbey and Palace of Holyrood were given to the flames. All along the east coast, and southwards as far as Merse and Teviotdale, marked the steps of the retreating and relentless invaders. Henry's savage instructions were faithfully carried out. When Hertford set out on this expedition he was commanded "to put all to fire and sword, to burn Edinburgh town, and to raze and deface it; when you have sacked it, and gotten what you can out of it, as that it may remain for ever a perpetual memory of the vengeance of God lighted upon it, for their falsehood and disloyalty. Do what you can out of hand, and without long tarrying, to beat down and overthrow the Castle, sack Holyrood-house, and as many towns and villages about Edinburgh as ye conveniently can; sack Leith and burn and subvert it, and all the rest, putting man, woman, and child to fire and sword, without exception, where any resistance shall be made against you; and this done, pass over to the Fife land, and extend the extremities and destructions in all towns and villages whereunto you may reach conveniently, and not forgetting amongst all the rest so to spoil and turn upside down the Cardinal's town of St. Andrews, as the upper stone may be the nether, and not one stick stand by another, sparing no creature alive within the same, specially such as in friendship or blood be allied to the Cardinal."

This hideous policy on the part of the English King was fruitful mainly of bitter memories. He did not accomplish the object he had in view, but he certainly succeeded in engendering in the Scottish mind a feeling of the most bitter hostility. It produced, however, one good result. It alienated from the English monarch some of those nobles who had for some time been wavering in their allegiance to the Scottish throne, and had been, either secretly or openly, lending their aid to further the machinations of the English government.

But destructive as Hertford's invasion proved (which has been well described as only a foray on a large scale), it was totally eclipsed by the raid undertaken by Sir Ralph Eure in the following year, 1544. He crossed the Scottish Border with a considerable army, and laid waste nearly the whole of Merse and Teviotdale, reducing that large and important district to a blackened desert. Jedburgh and Kelso were burnt to the ground, and the surrounding country plundered and destroyed. "The whole number of towns, towers, stedes, barnekins, parish churches, bastel-houses, seized, destroyed, and burnt, in all the Border country, was an hundred and ninety-two, Scots slain four hundred, prisoners taken eight hundred and sixteen, nolt ten thousand three hundred and eighty-six, sheep twelve thousand four hundred and ninety-six, gayts (goats) two hundred, bolls of corn eight hundred and fifty, insight gear—an indefinite quantity.

"The great part of these devastations were committed in the Mers and Teviotdale.... The other commanders of chief note, besides Sir Ralph Eure, were Sir Brian Laiton and Sir George Bowes. On the 17th July, Bowes, Laiton, and others burnt Dunse, the chief town of the Mers, and John Carr's son with his garrison entered Greenlaw, and carried off a booty of cattle, sheep, and horses. On the 19th of the same month, the men of Tyndale and Ridsdale, returning from a road into Tiviotdale, fought with the laird of Ferniherst and his company, and took himself and his son John prisoners. On July 24th the Wark garrison, the Captain of Norham Castle, and H. Eure, burnt long Ednim, made many prisoners, took a bastel-house strongly kept, and got a booty of forty nolt and thirty horses, besides those on which their prisoners were mounted, each on a horse. August 2d, the captain of Norham burnt the town of Home, hard to the castle gates, with the surrounding stedes. September 6th, Sir Ralph Eure burnt Eikford church and town, the barnekyn of Ormiston, and won by assault the Moss Tower, burnt it, and slew thirty-four people within it; he likewise burnt several other places in that neighbourhood, and carried off more than five hundred nolt and six hundred sheep, with a hundred horseload of spoils got in the tower. September 27th, the men of the east and part of the middle march won the church of Eccles by assault, and slew eight men in the abbey and town, most part gentlemen of head sirnames; they also took several prisoners, and burnt and spoiled the said abbey and town. On the same day the garrison of Berwick brought out of the east end of the Mers six hundred bolls of corn, and took prisoner Patrick Home, brother's son to the laird of Ayton. November 5th, the men of the middle march burnt Lessudden, in which were sixteen strong bastel-houses, slew several of the owners, and burnt much corn. November 9th, Sir George Bowes and Sir Brian Laiton burnt Dryburgh, a market town, all except the church, with much corn, and brought away a hundred nolt, sixty nags, an hundred sheep, and much other booty, spoilage, and insight-gear."

This record is an instructive one. It shows how these merciless raiders were dominated by the spirit of destruction and revenge. Nothing was spared which it was possible for them to destroy. This invasion must have proved peculiarly vexatious and disheartening to the Scottish Borderers. Flodden had left them terribly crippled. The damage they had sustained was not only of a material kind—the loss of men and resources—it was also, to a certain extent, moral and intellectual. They had become utterly disheartened, and it was some considerable time before they regained their wonted confidence and intrepidity:

"Dool and wae for the order, sent our lads to the Border!
The English, for ance, by guile wan the day:
The flowers of the forest, that fought aye the foremost,
The prime of our land, are cauld in the clay.

"We'll hear nae mair lilting, at the ewe milking;

Women and bairns are heartless and wae:
Sighing and moaning on ilka green loaning—
The flowers of the forest are a' wede awae."

The darkest part of the night precedes the dawn. Help was forthcoming from an unexpected quarter. Henry had promised to give Eure a grant of all the land he could conquer in Merse, Teviotdale, and Lauderdale, and it so happened that the greater part of the district named belonged to Angus, who was then in disgrace at the Scottish Court, and for some time had been currying favour with the English King. When he learned what had taken place, his indignation was unbounded. He swore that "if Ralph Eure dared to act upon the grant, he would write his sasine, or instrument of possession, on his skin with sharp pens and bloody ink." Scotland has not unfrequently been deserted by her nobles at the most critical periods of her history, but just as often has she been saved by their valour and patriotism. On the present occasion, Angus was not moved to action, perhaps, by any really patriotic feeling. Had his own interests not been imperilled, he would in all probability have remained an idle spectator of the ruin and devastation which, like a flood, was rushing over the land. Be this as it may, he acted with promptitude and effect. Having been joined by the Regent, who brought with him a small and hastily-gathered force, Angus challenged the English army at Melrose; and, though at first he was compelled to retreat, he hung upon the rear of the enemy until, joined by Sir Walter Scott of Buccleuch and the redoubtable Norman Leslie, he gave them battle on Ancrum Moor. The English, flushed with confidence by their former successes, rushed precipitately upon the Scottish army, believing that their ranks had fallen into confusion, and were preparing for flight. It was not long ere they were undeceived. The Scots were ready for the encounter, and in a short time completely routed the formidable host by which they were assailed. The battle speedily became a slaughter. Sir Ralph Eure and Sir Brian Layton both lay dead on the field, a thousand prisoners were taken, among them being many persons of rank, for whom high ransoms were exacted. It is said that the peasantry of the neighbourhood, hitherto only spectators of the short conflict, drew near to intercept and cut down the English; and women, whose hearts had been steeled against the fugitives by their atrocious barbarities, joined in the pursuit, and spurred on the conquerors by calling upon them to "remember Broomhouse." One of these heroines has been immortalized. Her monument may still be seen in the neighbourhood of Ancrum. On it were inscribed the following lines:—

"Fair maiden Lilliard lies under this stane,
Little was her stature, but great was her fame;
Upon the English loons she laid many thumps,
And when they cutted off her legs she fought upon her stumps."

Some may be disposed to think that the devastations caused by Hertford and Sir Ralph Eure must be exceptional; that the raiding and reiving must have gone on much more quietly than such accounts would lead us to suppose. But this is not so. The Borders were kept in a constant state of turmoil. They had no sooner recovered from one invasion than they were subjected to another. Long before Hertford's time, for example, Lord Dacre, one of the English wardens, made a succession of the most disastrous raids on the Scottish Border, and carried off immense quantities of booty. He was exultant over his good fortune. Writing under date October 29, 1513, he says:—"On Tewsday at night last past, I sent diverse of my tennents of Gillislande to the nombre of lx. personnes in Eskdalemoor upon the Middill Merches, and there brynt vii. howses, tooke and brougth away xxxvj. head of cattle and much insight. On weddinsday at thre of the clok efter noon, my broder Sir Christopher assembled diverse of the kings subjects beyng under my

27

reull, and roode all night into Scotland, and on Thurisday, in the mornynge, they began upon the said Middill Merchies and brynt Stakeheugh, with the hamletts belonging to them, down, Irewyn bwrne, being the chambrelain of Scotland owne lands and undre his reull, continewally birnyng from the Breke of day to oone of the clok after noon, and there wan, tooke and brought awey cccc. hede of cattell, ccc. shepe, certaine horses and verey miche insight, and slew two men, hurte and wounded diverse other persones and horses, and then entered Ingland ground again at vij. of the clok that night."

Such a record as this ought to have given great satisfaction to the Government. Lord Dacre had evidently done his utmost to impoverish and ruin the unfortunate Scottish Borderers. But the English appetite at this time was not easily satisfied. Naturally enough Dacre's invasion led to reprisals, and so successful had the Scots been in their forays on the opposite Border that the English Government blamed their representative for not having prevented these raids. In reply to these rather unjust complaints, Dacre wrote saying that "for oone cattell taken by the Scotts we have takyn, won and brought awey out of Scotland a hundreth; and for oone shepe two hundreth of a surity. And has for townships and housis, burnt in any of the said Est, Middill, and West Marches within my reull, fro the begynnyng of this warr unto this daye,... I assure your lordships for truthe that I have and hes caused to be burnt and distroyed sex times moo townys and howsys within the West and Middill Marches of Scotland, in the same season then is done to us, as I may be trusted, and as I shall evidently prove. For the watter of Liddall being xij. myles of length,... whereupon was a hundreth pleughs;... the watter of Ewse being viij. myles of length in the said Marches, whereupon was vii. pleughs,... lyes all and every of them waist now, noo corn sawn upon the said ground.... Upon the West marches I have burnt and distroyed the townships of Annand (together with thirty-three others mentioned in detail), and the Water of Esk from Stabulgorton down to Cannonby, being vi. myles in lenth, whereas there was in all tymes passed four hundreth ploughes and above, which are now clearly waisted and noo man duelling in any of them in this daye, save oonly in the towrys of Annand Steepel and Walghapp (Wauchope)."

As might be expected these inroads were not allowed to pass unredressed, as the Scots never missed an opportunity of retaliating. During the latter half of the fifteenth century they were considerably weakened by the successive wars in which they were compelled to engage in their own defence; but we find that a century later, during the reign of Elizabeth, they had completely recovered, and made their power felt in no uncertain manner. They raided upon the opposite Border without intermission, plundering all and sundry, sparing only those who were prepared to pay them blackmail, "that they might be free from their cumber." The English wardens were comparatively helpless, owing to their lack of men and horses to defend the Marches. The Scottish reivers were not easily captured; and when it came to an encounter, unless matched against a greatly superior force, they almost invariably gave a good account of themselves. We find Eure affirming, in a letter to Cecil, under date May, 1596, that the spoils of his March amounted to the sum of £120,000, "the redress for which is so cunningly delayed that the Queen's service is ruined." Sir Robert Cary, who was warden of the East March, has a still more doleful tale to relate. He says that when he applied to the opposite warden for redress he "got nothing but fair words." He furnished his Government with a note of the "slaughters, stouthes, and reafes," committed within his wardenry, which shows that the Scottish reivers were ever ready to make the most of their opportunities. The following is the suggestive list:—

"Nicolas Bolton of Mindrum slain in daylight at his own plough by Sir Robert Kerre of the Spielaw and his servants.

"Thomas Storie of Killam slain there by night by Sir Robert Kerre and his servants.

"John Selby of Pawston slain by the Burnes defending his own goods in his own house there.

"John Ewart of Corham slain on English ground at the rescue of Englishmen bringing their own goods.

"'Reafes.'—In Hethpoole in daylight by the Davisons, Yonges, and Burnes of 40 kyen and oxen, and hurting Thomas and Peter Storye, &c., in peril of their lives. Another there by daylight by the Kerres, Yonges, and Taites, of 46 head of neate, shooting John Gray with a 'peice' in peril of death, and hurting one of the Brewhouses following, and taking his horse. In West Newton in daylight by James Davidson of the Burnyrigge, &c., of 5 horse and mares; another there at night taking up 2 horses, 20 neate, and insight worth 20 nobles.

"On Thomas Routledge of Killam, at night, by the Yonges, of 30 kyen and oxen. On Adam Smith of Brigge mylle at night by the Kerres, Yonges, Burnes, &c., of 20 neate, and 5 horse and mares. In Cowpland, by the Yonges, Burnes, and Kerres on Gilbert Wright, 'by cutting up his doores with axes,' of 30 neate, 4 horses and mares, and insight worth £10. In Haggeston by the Yonges, Halles, Pyles, and Amysleyes, 'by cutting up their doores with axes,' of 30 neate, 5 naegs, and hunting 4 men in peril of death. On Ralph Selby, of West wood, by the Yonges, &c., 'by breaking his tower,' and taking 3 geldings worth £60 sterling 'and better.'"

Then follows a long list of "Stouthes," which it would only be a weariness to repeat. These incidents had all occurred in this March within a brief period, and may be accepted as an illustration of what was going on almost every day in the year within the respective wardenries. This game, it may be said, was indulged in with equal spirit and pertinacity on both sides. We read of two men in the Middle March in England coming into Liddesdale and carrying off 30 score kye and oxen, 31 score sheep and "gait," 24 horse and mares, and all their insight—"the people being at their schellis, lipning for no harme, and wounded twa puir men to their deid." At the same time, Captain Carvell, with 2000 "waigit" men, by Lord Scrope's special command, burnt "six myle of boundis in Liddisdale, tuik sindrie puir men and band them twa and twa in leisches and cordis, and that 'naikit,' taking awa a 1000 kye and oxen, 2000 sheep and 'sex scoir of hors and merris,' to the great wrak of the puir subjects."

These forays, it must be admitted, were sometimes conducted in the most relentless and cruel spirit. We read, for example, of one "Sowerby," near Coldbeck, having his house broken into, and himself most cruelly used. "They set him on his bare buttocks upon an hote iron, and then they burned him with an hote girdle about his bellie, and sundry other parts of his body, to make him give up his money, which they took, under £4."

Some of the most interesting episodes in Border history were not the outcome of any deep laid scheme, but the result of some sudden and unexpected emergency. It was difficult for the inhabitants of the opposite Marches to come into close contact without the greatest danger of an outbreak of hostilities. Individual families were often on friendly terms, and were ready even to assist each other on occasion. The Scots sometimes brought the English to help them to rob those who lived in their own neighbourhood; and the English, on the other hand, were equally ready to avail themselves of the assistance of those on the opposite Border when they had a similar object in view. But when they came together in their hundreds or thousands, as they sometimes did on a "Day of Truce," then it was a matter of supreme difficulty to keep them from flying at each other's throats. Feeling ran high, and a word, a look, was sometimes sufficient to change an otherwise peaceful meeting into one of turmoil and bloodshed.

One notable instance of this kind is known as the "Raid of the Reidswire." Sir John Foster, the English warden, and Sir John Carmichael, the warden on the opposite March, had a meeting for the regulation of Border affairs, on the 7th July, 1575. Each warden was attended by his retinue, and by the armed clans inhabiting the district. As the balladist describes it:

"Carmichael was our warden then,
He caused the country to convene;
And the Laird's Wat, that worthy man,
Brought in that sirname weil beseen:
The Armestranges, that aye ha'e been
A hardy house, but not a hail,
The Elliots' honours to maintaine,
Brought down the lave o' Liddisdale.

"Then Tividale came to wi' spied;
The Sheriffe brought the Douglas down,
Wi' Cranstane, Gladstain, good at need,
Baith Rewle water and Hawick town,
Beanjeddart bauldly made him boun,
Wi' a' the Trumbills, strong and stout;
The Rutherfoords with grit renown,
Convoy'd the town of Jedbrugh out."

The two parties had apparently met on the best of terms. Mirth and good fellowship prevailed. The pedlars erected their temporary booths, and sold their wares. The gathering presented the appearance of a rural fair. No one could have suspected that so much bad feeling was hidden under such a fair exterior, and ready to burst forth in a moment with volcanic fury. Yet such was the case. A dispute arose betwixt the two wardens about one Farnsteen, a notorious English freebooter, against whom a bill had been "filed" by a Scottish complainer. Foster declared that he had fled from justice, and could not be found. Carmichael regarded this statement as a pretext to avoid making compensation for the felony. He bade Foster "play fair." The English warden was indignant. Raising himself in the saddle, and stretching his arm in the direction of Carmichael, he told him to match himself with his equals!

"Carmichael bade them speik out plainlie,
And cloke no cause for ill nor good;
The other, answering him as vainlie,
Began to reckon kin and blood:

He raise, and raxed him where he stood,
And bade him match with him his marrows;
Then Tindaill heard them reason rude,
And they loot off a flight of arrows."

The cry was raised, "To it, Tynedale," and immediately the merry meeting was turned into a Donnybrook fair, where hard blows were given and received. The Scots at first had the worst of the encounter, and would have been completely routed had it not been for two circumstances. The men of Tynedale, conscious of their superior strength, began to rifle the "merchant packs," and thus fell into disorder. At this juncture a band of citizens of Jedburgh, armed with fire-arms, unexpectedly, but most opportunely, appeared on the scene, and in a short time the skirmish ended in a complete victory for the Scots. Sir John Heron was slain, and Sir John Foster and many other Englishmen of rank taken prisoner.

"But after they had turned backs,
Yet Tindaill men they turn'd again,
And had not been the merchant packs,
There had been mae of Scotland slain.

But, Jesu! if the folks were fain
To put the bussing on their thies;
And so they fled, wi' a' their main,
Down ower the brae, like clogged bees."

The prisoners were sent to Dalkeith, where for a short time they were detained in custody by the Earl of Morton. He ultimately dismissed them with presents of falcons, which gave rise to a saying on the Borders that for once the Regent had lost by his bargain, as he had given live hawks for dead herons,—alluding to the death of Sir John Heron.

"Who did invent that day of play,
We need not fear to find him soon;
For Sir John Forster, I dare well say,
Made us this noisome afternoon.
Not that I speak preceislie out,
That he supposed it would be perril;
But pride, and breaking out of feuid
Garr'd Tindaill lads begin the quarrel."

"The Queen of England," says Ridpath, "when informed of these proceedings, was very much incensed, and sent orders to her Ambassador, Killigrew, who had a little before gone to Scotland, to demand immediate satisfaction for so great an outrage. Killigrew was also directed to inform the Regent that the Queen had ordered the Earl of Huntingdon, who was then president of the Council at York and lieutenant of the northern counties, to repair to the Borders for the trial and ordering of the matter; and that she expected that Morton would meet him in person for that effect. Morton, ever studious to gratify Elizabeth, readily agreed to the proposal. The two Earls accordingly met at Fouldean, near the Berwick boundary, and continued their conferences there for some days, in the course of which Morton made such concessions, and agreed to such conditions of redress, as entirely healed the offence. Carmichael, who was considered as the principal offender, was sent as a prisoner into England, and detained a few weeks at York; but the English Court being now convinced that Forrester had been in the wrong in the beginning of the fray, the Scottish warden was dismissed with honour, and gratified with a present to effectuate the restitution of goods which Morton had engaged should be made by the subjects of Scotland, he summoned all on this side of the Forth to attend him with twenty days' provision of victuals in an expedition to the Borders, but this summons sufficed to awe the offenders to make of themselves the restitution required."

V

THE WARDENS OF THE MARCHES.

"The widdefow wardanis tuik my geir,
And left me nowthir horse nor meir,
Nor erdly guid that me belangit;
Now, walloway! I mon be hangit."

Pinkerton.

wing to the peculiar circumstances in which the Borders were placed, it was found necessary, for the preservation of order, and the detection and punishment of crime, to appoint special officers, or wardens, armed with the most extensive powers. On either side of the Border there were three Marches, lying opposite each other, called the East, West, and Middle Marches. The wardens were, as a general rule, officers of high rank, holding special commissions from the Crown. The English government had little difficulty in finding gentlemen of high station and proved ability to undertake the duties of such an office; but in Scotland the King was considerably circumscribed in his choice, as the Border Chiefs were accustomed to carry things with a high hand, and in any arrangements relating to the management of affairs in their own districts, their wishes and interests had, perforce, to be respected. The office of warden was regarded as belonging, by a kind of prescriptive or hereditary right, to one or other of the more prominent and powerful Border families. This policy was fraught with many disadvantages, and, it must be frankly admitted, produced the very evils it was designed to suppress. The Scottish wardens had other objects in view besides the maintenance of a certain semblance of law and order in the districts over which they ruled. They seldom lost sight of their own pecuniary interests, and frequently prostituted their high office to secure their own ends. The wardens themselves were often the principal offenders.

In the East March the warden was most generally either an Earl of Home or a Ker of Cessford. The Middle March was long under the supervision of the Earls of Bothwell and the Lords of Buccleuch. The West March was usually represented either by a Johnstone or a Maxwell.

The Scottish wardens, though invested with the most arbitrary powers, found it politic to enter into bonds of alliance with the neighbouring Chiefs, in order not only to increase their influence and power within their own wardenries, but to add to their authority when called upon to deal with questions of a more general nature. This fact reveals unmistakably the weakness of the central government of the country at this period, and indicates the important part which was played by the nobility in the administration of the affairs of the nation.

Several of these "Bonds" have been preserved. Some of them are too lengthy for quotation, but the following one—which is comparatively brief—may be taken as a fair sample of the whole. It is subscribed by the Lairds of Buccleuch, Hunthill, Bon-Jeddart, Greenhead, Cavers, and Redheugh, in favour of Sir Thomas Ker of Fernihirst, and runs as follows:—"We undersigned, inhabitants of the Middle March of this realm opposite England, understanding how it has pleased the King's majesty our sovereign lord to make and constitute Sir Thomas Ker of Fernihirst Knight his Highness warden and justice over all the Middle March, and acknowledging how far we are in duty bound to the service by our counsel and forces to be employed in the assistance of his said warden in all things tending to the good rule and quietness of the said Middle March, and setting forth of his Highness authority against these traitors, rebels, and other malefactors to their due punishment, and defence and safety of true men. Therefore we be bound and obliged, and by the tenor hereof binds and obliges us, and every one of us, that we should truly serve the King's Majesty our sovereign lord, and obey and assist his said warden, in the premiss, and shall concur with others in giving of our advice and counsel, or with our forces in pursuit or defence of the said thieves, traitors, rebels, and other malefactors disobedient to our sovereign lord's authority, or disturbers of the public peace and quietness of the realm, as we shall be charged or warned by open proclamations, missives, bailies, or other the like accustomed forms as we will answer to his Highness upon our obedience at our highest charge and peril, if we shall be found remiss or negligent, we are content to be repute held and esteemed as favourers and partakers with the said thieves, traitors, rebels, and malefactors in their treasonable and wicked deeds, and to be called, pursued, and punished therefor, according to these laws in example of others."

There can be no doubt that these "Bonds" were often contracted in good faith; that is to say, those who subscribed them were honestly desirous to fulfil, both in the spirit and letter, the obligations thus undertaken. It is, however, worthy of remark that those who had thus sworn allegiance to the warden had not infrequently ends of their own to serve, which conflicted with their duty to the representatives of law and order. Thieves were harboured, or at least allowed to remain unmolested, on the estates, or within the jurisdiction, of those who had thus professedly banded themselves together for their detection and punishment. The result was that the subscribers to the "Bond" were occasionally reported to the government for their delinquencies, and prosecuted and punished for their breach of faith. Thus we find that on one occasion Walter Ker of Cessford, James Douglas of Cavers, George Rutherford of Hunthill, and Ker of Dolphingstone were convicted of art and part of the favour and assistance afforded to Robert Rutherford, called Cokburn, and John Rutherford, called Jok of the Green, and their accomplices, rebels and at the horn; permitting them to pass within their bounds continually for divers years past; for not using their utmost endeavour to hinder them from committing sundry slaughters, stouth-reifs, thefts and oppressions on the King's poor lieges, nor ejecting the said rebels, their wives and their children, from their bounds and bailiaries, but knowingly suffering them to pass within their limits and to remain therein beyond the space of twelve hours, to commit sundry crimes during the time of their passing and reset within the shire in which they dwelt, thereby breaking, transgressing, and violating their obligation and "Bond" to the King, and incurring the pains contained in the said "Bond."

It is remarkable, considering the reputation enjoyed by the Borderers for being true to their word, that such occurrences should have to be so frequently complained of.

Unfortunately, the wardens were as little animated by a high sense of honour as those who had solemnly pledged themselves to support them in the discharge of the duties of their office. They frequently, and in some cases almost systematically, exercised the powers conferred on them, not in trying to preserve the public peace, but in wreaking vengeance on their enemies. A striking instance of this is to be seen in the conflict which was so long waged between the Johnstones and the Maxwells, and which produced endless misery and mischief throughout a wide area.

All things considered, the wardens were well remunerated for such services as they were able to render. The usual fee appears to have been £100 per annum. In 1527 the Earl of Angus had £100 for the East and a similar sum for the Middle March. In 1553 the Warden's fee was £500, but he had to surrender the one half of the "escheats" to the authorities. When William Ker of Cessford was appointed warden of the Middle March and keeper of Liddesdale, his salary for the former office was £100, and for the latter £500. But these sums represented but a small part of the actual income. They were also allowed forage and provision for their retinue, which consisted of a guard of horsemen. They had in addition a portion of the "unlaws" or fines imposed in the warden courts, and at certain periods these must have amounted to a large sum. The law ordained that "the escheat of all thieves and trespassers that are convict of their movable goods, ought and should pertain to the warden for his travail and labours, to be used and disposed by him at his pleasure in time coming. The warden ought and should take and apprehend all and sundry our sovereign Lord's lieges turning and carrying nolt, sheep, horses, or victuals furth of this realm into England, and bring their persons to the King's justice, to be punished therefor; and all their goods may he escheat: the one half thereof to be applied to the King's use, and the other half to the warden for his pains." In addition to this, the wardens had a large share of the plunder of the various forays upon the English Border, which they either conducted in person, or winked at when undertaken by their retainers or dependants. In the "Border Papers" we are informed that on Sunday, the 17th April, 1597, the Lord Buccleuch, Keeper of Liddesdale, accompanied by twenty horse and a hundred foot, burned at noonday three onsets and dwelling-houses, barns, stables, oxhouses, &c., to the number of twenty, in the head of Tyne, cruelly burning in their houses seven innocent men, and "murdered with the sword" fourteen which had been in Scotland, and brought away the booty, the head officer with trumpet being there in person This was a frequent occurrence, especially with Buccleuch, who was never quite happy when not plundering and oppressing "the auld enemy." From a pecuniary point of view, not to speak of other advantages, the office of warden was a highly desirable one, and was consequently eagerly sought after by the Border Chiefs.

The duties pertaining to this office may be described as of a twofold nature—the maintenance of law and order, and the protection of the districts against the encroachments and inroads of the enemy. "In the first capacity," as has been remarked, "besides their power of control and ministerial administration, both as head stewards of all the crown tenements and manors within their jurisdiction, and as intromitting with all fines and penalties, their judicial authority was very extensive. They held courts for punishment of high treason and felony, which the English Border laws classed under the following heads:—

I. The aiding and abetting of any Scottishman, by communing, appointment, or otherwise, to rob, burn, or steal, within the realm of England.

II. The accompanying personally, of any Scottishman, while perpetrating any such offences.

III. The harbouring, concealing, or affording guidance and protection to him after the fact.

IV. The supplying Scottishmen with arms and artillery, as jacks, splents, brigantines, coats of plate, bills, halberds, battle-axes, bows and arrows, spears, darts, guns, as serpentines, half-haggs, harquibusses, currys, cullivers, hand-guns, or daggers, without special licence of the Lord-warden.

V. The selling of bread and corn of any kind, or of dressed leather, iron, or other appurtenances belonging to armour, without special licence.

VI. The selling of horses, mares, nags, or geldings to Scottish men, without licence as aforesaid.

VII. The breach of truce, by killing or assaulting subjects and liege-men of Scotland.

VIII. The assaulting of any Scottishman having a regular pass or safe-conduct.

IX. In time of war the giving tidings to the Scottish of any exploit intended against them by the warden or his officers.

X. The conveying coined money, silver or gold, also plate or bullion, into Scotland, above the value of forty shillings at one time.

XI. The betraying (in time of war) the counsel of any other Englishman tending to the annoyance of Scotland, in malice to the party, and for his own private advantage.

XII. The forging the coin of the realm.

XIII. The making appointment and holding communication with Scotchmen, or intermarrying with a Scottish woman, without licence of the wardens, and the raising of no fray against them as in duty bound.

XIV. The receiving of Scottish pilgrims with their property without licence of the wardens.

XV. The failing to keep the watches appointed for the defence of the country.

XVI. The neglecting to raise in arms to the fray, or alarm raised by the wardens or watches upon the approach of public danger.

XVII. The receiving or harbouring Scottish fugitives exiled from their own country for misdemeanours.

XVIII. The having falsely and unjustly *fould* (*i.e.*, found true and relevant) the bill of any Scotchman against an Englishman, or having borne false witness on such matters.

XIX. The having interrupted or stopped any Englishman pursuing for recovering of his stolen goods.

XX. The dismissing any Scottish offender taken red-hand (*i.e.*, in the manner) without special license of the Lord-warden.

XXI. The paying of black-mail, or protection money, whether to English or Scottish man."

The significance of these provisions cannot be mistaken. They reveal the anxiety of the English government to prevent, as far as possible, all intercourse with Scottish Borderers. The offences referred to in the foregoing list amounted to what is known as March Treason. Those who were accused of this crime were tried by a jury, and if found guilty were put to death without ceremony. "This was a very ordinary consummation," says Sir Walter Scott, "if we can believe a story told of Lord William Howard of Naworth. While busied deeply with his studies, he was suddenly disturbed by an officer who came to ask his commands concerning the disposal of several moss-troopers who had just been made prisoners. Displeased at the interruption, the warden answered heedlessly and angrily, 'hang them in the devil's name;' but when he laid aside his book, his surprise was not little, and his regret considerable, to find that his orders had been literally fulfilled."

The duties devolving upon the Scottish wardens were not, in all respects, the same as those which the English wardens were called upon to discharge. This was due to some extent to the fact that the jurisdiction of the Scottish wardens was circumscribed by the hereditary rights and privileges of the great families who, within their own territories, exercised supreme control. In addition to this, the hereditary judges had the power of repledging; that is to say, they could reclaim any accused person from courts of co-ordinate jurisdiction, and try him by their feudal authority. But while the power of the wardens was thus considerably circumscribed, they never hesitated, when they had the chance, to mete out summary punishment to all offenders. If a thief was caught red-handed, or if the evidence against him appeared at all conclusive, he was at once, and without ceremony, strung up on the nearest tree, or thrown into the "murder" pit. Indeed, the execution not unfrequently preceded the trial—a circumstance which seems to have given rise to the well-know proverb about "Jeddart Justice." On both sides of the Border, the same haste to get rid of offenders was a noted feature of the times. This is evident from the well-known English proverb which runs thus—

"I oft have heard of Lydford law,
Where in the morn men hang and draw,
And sit in judgment after."

The sitting in judgment, either before or after, was a formality that might often have been dispensed with, as the evidence submitted was seldom carefully sifted, or weighed. To be suspected, or accused, was regarded as almost tantamount to a plea of guilty. Such a method as this would hardly pass muster in our modern and more finical age; still it is probable that substantial justice was usually done. If those who were condemned were not always guilty of the particular crimes laid to their charge, their general record was sufficiently bad to warrant their being thus summarily dealt with.

There was, moreover, a practical difficulty in the way of minute investigation being made into each individual case. The number of those accused of various offences under the Border laws was often so great as to render an investigation of this kind all but impossible. There were few places of strength where prisoners could be retained in order to await their trial, and so it became necessary to deal with them as expeditiously as possible. "The Borderers," it has been said, "were accustomed to part with life with as little form as civilized men change their garments."

The mode of punishment was either by hanging or drowning. "Drowning," says Sir Walter Scott, "is a very old mode of punishment in Scotland, and in Galloway there were pits of great depth appropriated to that punishment still called murder-holes, out of which human bones have occasionally been taken in great quantities. This points out the proper interpretation of the right of 'pit and gallows' (in law Latin, *fossa et furca*), which has, less probably, been supposed the right of imprisoning in the pit or dungeon, and that of hanging. But the meanest baron possessed the right of imprisonment. The real meaning is, the right of inflicting death either by hanging or drowning."

But the warden had other duties to discharge of a still more important nature than those already described. In time of war he was captain-general within his own wardenry, and was invested with the power of calling musters of all the able-bodied men between the age of sixteen and sixty. These men were suitably armed and mounted according to their rank and condition, and were expected to be ready either to defend their territory against invasion, or, if necessary, to invade the enemy's country. The ancient rights and customs which the warden was expected to observe on such occasion have been thus summarised:—

"I. All intercourse with the enemy was prohibited.

II. Any one leaving the company during the time of the expedition was liable to be punished as a traitor.

III. It was appointed that all should alight and fight on foot, except those commanded by the general to act as cavalry.

IV. No man was to disturb those appointed to array the host.

V. If a soldier followed the chase on a horse belonging to his comrade, the owner of the horse enjoyed half the booty; and if he fled upon such a horse, it was to be delivered to the sheriff as a waif on his return home, under pain of treason.

VI. He that left the host after victory, though for the purpose of securing his prisoner, lost his ransom.

VII. Any one seizing his comrade's prisoner was obliged to find security in the hands of the warden-serjeant. Disputed prisoners were to be placed in the hands of the warden, and the party found ultimately wrong to be amerced in a fine of ten pounds.

VIII. Relates to the evidence in case of such dispute. He who could bring his own countrymen in evidence, of whatsoever quality, was preferred as the true captor; failing this mode of proof, recourse was had to the prisoner's oath.

IX. If the prisoner was of such a rank as to lead a hundred men, he was either to be dismissed upon security or ransomed, for the space of fifteen days, without leave of the warden.

X. He who dismounted a prisoner was entitled to half of his ransom.

XI. Whosoever detected a traitor was entitled to a reward of one hundred shillings; whoever aided his escape, suffered the pain of death.

XII. Relates to the firing of beacons in Scotland: the stewards of Annandale and Kirkcudbright were liable in the fine of one merk for each default in the matter.

XIII. He who did not join the army of the country upon the signal of the beacon lights, or who left it during the English invasion without lawful excuse, his goods were forfeited, and his person placed at the warden's will.

XIV. In the case of any Englishman being taken in Scotland, he was not suffered to depart under any safe conduct save that of the King or warden; and a similar protection was necessary to enable him to return and treat of his ransom.

XV. Any Scottishman dismissing his prisoner, when a host was collected either to enter England or defend against invasion, was punished as a traitor.

XVI. In the partition of spoil, two portions were allowed to each bowman.

XVII. Whoever deserted his commander and comrades, and abode not in the field to the uttermost, his goods were forfeited, and his person liable to punishment as a traitor.

XVIII. Whoever bereft his comrade of horse, spoil, or prisoner, was liable in the pains of treason, if he did not make restitution after the right of property became known to him."

These military regulations, at once minute and comprehensive, were drawn up by William, Earl of Douglas, with the assistance of some of the most experienced Marchmen; and, with the necessary alterations, were adopted by the English—thus indicating that they were thoroughly in harmony with the military spirit of the age on both sides of the Border.

VI.

THE DAY OF TRUCE.

"Our wardens they affixed the day,
And as they promised so they met.
Alas! that day I'll ne'er forget!"

Old Ballad.

The arrangements made for dealing with offences against Border law, though of a primitive, were by no means of an ineffective, character. All things considered, they were perhaps as good as could have been devised in the circumstances. During the period when Border reiving was most rampant, though the population was by no means sparse, little or no provision had been made for detaining prisoners in custody.

The jails were few and far between, and such as were available were generally in such an insecure and ruinous state that, unless strongly guarded, they were almost useless for the purpose for which they existed. But imprisonment had other inconveniences which militated against its being resorted to with much frequency. Prisoners had to be provided for when under "lock and key," and, as provisions were difficult to procure, it was generally found more advantageous to leave those who had broken the laws to "fend" for themselves until such times as they were wanted. As might be expected in such circumstances, the accused person not unfrequently took "leg-bail," and passed into another district, or, perhaps, crossed the Border, and sought refuge among the enemies of his country and his clan. This expedient, in those lawless and disordered times, was no doubt occasionally successful—for the nonce—but sooner or later the evil-doer was either betrayed by the enemy, or, resuming his old habits—which was almost a necessity—brought himself under the special notice of the warden of the district to which he had fled. He thus placed himself, as it were, between two fires, and made further immunity from prosecution practically impossible. When it came to the knowledge of the warden that an accused person had passed into another wardenry, he at once certified the warden opposite, requiring him to apprehend and deliver the prisoner with all possible speed; and he was bound, after receiving this notice, to make proclamation throughout his wardenry "by the space of six days after of the said fugitive," and also to certify the other two wardens of the realm "to proclaim the fugitive throughout all the bounds of their wardenries, so that none could proclaim ignorance, or excuse themselves when charged with the wilful receipt of the aforesaid fugitive so proclaimed."

The duty thus laid upon the wardens of searching for fugitives was one which was generally undertaken *con amore*, not merely on account of the fact that it was naturally agreeable to these officers to detect and punish crime, but also because in such circumstances it was greatly to their advantage to do so. A law was passed ordaining that when a fugitive entered with his goods into the opposite realm, the warden who captured him, and handed him over to be punished for his offence, *was entitled to retain the goods for his labour*. Should he not succeed in apprehending the fugitive, then the goods had to be returned to the warden of the realm from which they came. This was a wise arrangement, and on the whole proved fairly effective.

As offences against the law were numerous and frequent, it was statute and ordained that a "Day of Truce" should be held every month, or oftener, when the wardens of the Marches opposite each other should meet for the discussion and adjustment of their respective claims, and the punishment of evil-doers. The date and place of this meeting was made known to the inhabitants of the Marches by proclamation being made in all the market towns. Notice was also sent to the lords, knights, esquires, and gentlemen, commanding them, along with a sufficient number of their tenants and servants, well mounted and fully armed, to repair the night before and attend upon the warden at the day of truce.

Early on the morning of the following day this imposing cavalcade might be seen wending its way towards the place of rendezvous. This was generally some convenient spot near the Border, most frequently on the Scottish side. When the wardens and their friends came within hailing distance of each other, a halt was called, and the English warden sent forward four or five gentlemen of good repute to demand from the Scottish warden "that assurance might be kept" until the sunrise of the following day. According to a statement made on the authority of Sir Robert Bowes, the reason of this particular form of procedure was "because the Scots did always send their ambassadors first into England to seek for peace after a war. Therefore both the particular days of truce are usually kept either at places even on the confines of the Marches, or else at places within the realm of Scotland, and also the English warden and other officers were always used to send first for the assurance as aforesaid."

When assurance had been given by the Scottish warden, a number of Scottish gentlemen passed over to the other side to demand from the English warden assurance on his part. These preliminary precautions having been duly observed, the two parties met, and the business which had brought them together was at once entered upon. The wardens did not always attend these meetings in person, their duties occasionally necessitating their remaining at home, but when unable to be present themselves they were represented by deputies—men of influence and good social position—who were thoroughly qualified to deal with any important question that might arise.

The regulations for the conduct of business at these meetings were carefully drawn out, and, as a general rule, strictly observed. The English warden named six Scottish gentlemen to act on his side, and the Scottish warden the same number of Englishmen to act as the English assize. These men, who thus constituted the jury, were carefully chosen. No murderer, traitor, fugitive, infamous person, or betrayer of one party to another could bear office, or give evidence, but only good and lawful men deserving of credit and unsuspected.

Each warden, in the presence of the opposite warden and the inhabitants of both the Marches, "Swore by the High God that reigneth above all Kings and Realms, and to whom all Christians owe obedience, that he shall (in the name of God) do, exercise and use his office without respect of person, Malice, Favour, or Affection, diligently or undelayedly, according to his Vocation or Charge that he beareth under God and his Prince, and he shall do justice upon all Complaints presented unto him, upon every Person complained upon under this Rule. And that, when any complaint is referred unto him, to swear, fyle, and deliver upon his Honour, he shall search, enquire, and redress the same at his uttermost power: And that, if it shall happen in so doing to quit and absolve the persons complained upon as Clean and Innocent: Yet if he shall any ways get sure Knowledge of the very Offender, he shall declare him foul of the Offence, and make lawful Redress and Delivery thereof, albeit the very Offender be not named in the Complaint: And this Oath of the Wardens not only to be made at the first Meeting hereafter to ensue, but also to be made every Year once solemnly, as aforesaid, at the first Meeting after *Mid-summer*, to put them in the better Remembrance of their Duties, and to place the fear of God in their Hearts."

The following oath was also administered to the jury:—"Ye shall truly enquire, and true deliverance make between the Queen's Majesty, and the prisoners at the Bar, according to the evidence that shall be given in this Court. As God keep you and Holydome."

These formalities having been duly observed, the trial of the prisoners was then proceeded with. Bills were presented on the one side, and on the other, setting forth with considerable fulness of detail the nature and extent of the damages that had been sustained. The prisoners against whom these indictments had been made were then called to answer the charges preferred against them.

There were at least three ways in which these cases could be tried. In the first place, the bill might be acquitted *on the honour of the warden*. But should it afterwards be found that the warden in acquitting the bill had proceeded on imperfect information, and had acquitted upon his honour a bill that was in reality "foul," then the complainant was at liberty to prosecute a new bill, and demand that justice should be done. The case was then tried by a jury who "fyled" or "cleared" the bill at their discretion. When a bill was "fyled," that is to say declared true, the word "foul" was written on the margin, and when it was "cleared," the word "clear" was inserted.

But further, bills might be *tried by inquest or assize*, which was the method most frequently adopted, such cases being decided by the juries on their own knowledge, and on the evidence sworn to in open court.

The third way of dealing with bills was by a "*Vower*." The significance of this method is fully explained by Sir Robert Bowes, who says:—"The inquest or assise of Scotlande, notwithstanding their othe, would in no wyse fynde a bill to be true, nor fyll any Scottis man upon an Englishman's complaynte unles the Englishman could fynde an inhabitant of Scotlande, that would avow openly to the inquest, or secretlye to the warden, or some of the inquest, that the complaynte was treue, and the partie complayned upon culpable thereof, otherwise althoughe the matter was ever so notoryously knowne by the Englishman, their evydence would not serve to secure a conviction."

It frequently happened, on the occasion of these meetings, that "bogus" bills were presented, a custom which gave the officials a great deal of unnecessary labour. The commissioners, in referring to this reprehensible practice, remark that "it hath been perceived of late that, since the order was begun by the Warden to speire, fyle, and deliver, upon their Honour, that some ungodly Persons have made complaint, and billed for Goods lost where none was taken from them, and so troubled the Wardens, causing them to speire and search for the Thing that was never done." It was therefore statute and ordained that all persons guilty of this offence should be delivered to the opposite warden to be punished, imprisoned, and fined at the discretion of the same warden whom he had troubled.

Another formidable difficulty with which the wardens had to contend on these occasions, was in estimating the value of the goods for which redress was claimed. In making up a bill the complainant was strongly tempted to put an absurd value on the gear, or cattle, which had been stolen from him. Had he always got as much as he claimed he would soon have been enormously enriched by the loss of his property! The commissioners were therefore under the necessity of drawing out a scale of charges for the guidance of the warden courts. The following are the prices fixed by this tribunal:— "Every Ox, above Four Year old, Fourty Shillings Sterling; every Cow, above Four Year old, Thirty Shillings Sterling; and every Young Cow, above Two Years old, Twenty Shillings Sterling; every other Beast, under Two Years old, Ten Shillings Sterling; every old Sheep, Six Shillings Sterling; and every Sheephogge, Three Shillings Sterling; every old Swine, above One Year old, Six Shillings Sterling; every young Swine, Two Shillings Sterling; every Goat, above One Year old, Five Shillings Sterling; every young Goat, Two Shillings Sterling; and every Double Toope to be valued after the rate of the Single."

These prices, judged by the standard of the present day, seem absurdly low, but they may be accepted as representing the average rate of prices obtainable, three hundred years ago, for the various classes of stock mentioned.

It was the duty of the wardens to have the offenders in custody, against whom bills had been presented, in readiness to answer, and in case the bills were "fouled" he was bound to deliver them up to the opposite warden, by whom they were imprisoned until they had paid a *single and two doubles*, that is to say, treble the value of the estimated goods in the bill. To produce these men was generally the most difficult part of the warden's duty. He could not keep them in confinement until the day of truce, for, independently they were sometimes persons of power and rank, their numbers were too great to be retained in custody. The wardens, therefore, usually took bonds from the Chief, kinsmen, or allies of the accused party, binding him or them to enter him prisoner within the iron gate of the warden's castle, or else to make him forthcoming when called for. He against whom a bill was twice fouled, was liable to the penalty of death. If the offender endeavoured to rescue himself after being lawfully delivered over to the opposite warden, he was liable to the punishment of death, or otherwise at the warden's pleasure, as being guilty of a breach of the assurance.

It would seem to have been customary on a day of truce to enumerate the various bills "fouled" on either side, and then to strike a balance, showing on which side most depredations had been committed. It occasionally happened that the claims of both parties were so numerous and complicated, the same person frequently appearing both as plaintiff and defendant, that it was deemed prudent to draw a veil over the whole proceedings, and give satisfaction to neither party, thus wiping out, as it were, with a stroke of the pen, and without further parleying, all the claims which had been lodged. This mode of procedure, arbitrary though it may appear, did not, as a rule, result in serious injustice being done to either party.

The offences dealt with were of a varied character. Reiving was only one of the many ways in which the Borderers sought to enrich themselves at the expense of their neighbours in the opposite March. They had an eye to the land as well as to the cattle. It was customary for them not only to pasture their stock on the enemy's territory, but to sow corn, cut down wood, and go hunting and hawking for pleasure as well as profit. Sir Robert Cary, one of the most vigorous of the English wardens, was determined that hunting without leave should not be carried on in his wardenry. He wrote to the laird of Fernihest, the warden opposite, explaining his views, but, "notwithstanding this letter," he says, "within a month after they came and hunted as they used to do without leave, and cut down wood and carried it away. I wrote to the warden, and told him I would not suffer one other affront, but if they came again without leave they would dearly aby it. For all this they would not be warned; but towards the end of the summer they came again to their wonted sports. I sent my two deputies with all speed they could make, and they took along with them such gentlemen as were in their way, with my forty horse, and about one of the clock they came to them, and set upon them; some hurt was done, but I gave special order they should do as little hurt, and shed as little blood, as they possibly could. They observed my command, only they broke all their carts, and took a dozen of the principal gentlemen that were there, and brought them to me to Witherington, where I lay. I made them welcome, and gave them the best entertainment I could. They lay in the castle two or three days, and so I sent them home—they assuring me that they would never again hunt without leave, which they did truly perform all the time."

This firm, but kindly method, was entirely satisfactory; and, had the Borders only been blessed with a succession of Carys in the various wardenries, the probability is that Border reiving would never have attained such portentous dimensions.

But despite the masterful management of men like Cary, such questions as those we have mentioned continued to occupy the time and attention of the warden courts. The freebooters on the Border never considered too closely the minute shades of difference between *meum* and *tuum*, and were difficult to persuade that depasturing, or cutting wood in a neighbour's plantation, was a matter of any real importance. They were at all times disposed to put a liberal construction on the words—"The earth is the Lord's and the fulness thereof." Their somewhat loose interpretation of this ancient Hebrew maxim occasioned them no end of vexation and trouble.

But the settlement of Border affairs on the day of truce did not interfere with the ancient custom which entitled the person who was robbed to follow his goods on what was called the *hot-trod*, and mete out summary punishment to the offender—provided he could overtake him. The warden also was enjoined, in the Act of 1563, to pursue and chase in hot-trod, unto such time or place as the fugitives or offender be apprehended, to bring him again within his own jurisdiction to be punished for the offence, "as appertaineth;" "and that without let, trouble, or impediment to be made or done to him by any of the inhabitants of that realm wherein he pursueth." And if any person should make resistance to the said warden in the foresaid pursuit he was to be billed for, and delivered to the warden. In the following of the said chase, in the manner aforesaid, it was thought convenient, and ordained, that the pursuer shall, at the first town he cometh by of the opposite realm, or the first person he meeteth with, give knowledge of the occasion of his chase, and require him to go with him in the said pursuit. If the offender was caught red-handed he was executed; but if the desire for gain was stronger than the thirst for blood, then he was held at ransom. The prey was followed with hound and horn, hue and cry, the pursuers carrying on the point of their spears a lighted piece of turf.

The business of the warden courts was conducted with despatch. When all the bills had been either "fouled" or "cleared," those who had been found guilty of "March Treason" were brought up for sentence. The lord warden called on him whose office it was to see the prisoners suffer, and thus addressed him:—"I command you in the Queen's Majesty's name that ye see execution done upon these prisoners, according to the Law of the Marches, at your peril." Then addressing the prisoners he said:—"Ye that are adjudged by the Law of the Realm to die, remember that ye have but a short time to live in this world; therefore earnestly call to God, with penitent hearts, for mercy and forgiveness of your sinful lives; repent ye have broken God's commandments, and be sorry therefor, and for that ye did not fear the breach and dangers of the Law, therefore your bodies must suffer the pain of death, provided to satisfy the reward of your Fact in this world; yet the salvation of your soul's health for the world to come, stands in the great mercy of Almighty God: Wherefore do ye earnestly repent and ask mercy for your sins, now when ye are living, put your Trust to be saved by the merits of Christ's passion; and think in your hearts if ye were able to recompence them ye have offended, ye would do it; and where you are not able, ask Forgiveness. Have such faith in God's Mercy as Dismas the Thief and Man-Murderer had that hang at Christ's Right hand, when he suffered his Passion for the Redemption of Mankind: Whose Faith was so great he should be saved, his Sins were remitted, tho' he had but short time of Repentance, and he enjoyed Heaven. Therefore despair not in God's Mercy, though your sins be great, for God's Mercy exceedeth all his Works. Set apart all Vanities of this World, and comfort you in Heavenly things; and doubt not but, if ye so do, ye shall inherit Everlasting Joy in the Kingdom of Heaven. And thus I commit you to the Mercy of God, wishing your Deaths may be an Example to all Parents to bring up their Children in the Fear of God, and Obedience of the Laws of this Realm."

With these suitable admonitions ringing in their ears, the condemned prisoners were led forth to execution.

The business of the court having been finished, the wardens retired after taking a courteous leave of each other.

These meetings, attended as they were by a large number of people, who came either on business or pleasure, were frequently broken up by sudden outbursts of tumult and disorder. *Baughling*, or brawling, was a common occurrence, and loud words and angry looks naturally led to more serious encounters. We have already noticed the incident of the Reidswire, but this was by no means an isolated case. In the month of July, 1585, at a day of truce between Sir John Foster and Ker of Ferniherst, Lord Russell, a young man of great promise, and of the most amiable disposition, was suddenly shot dead by an unknown hand. This lamentable incident gave rise to much bitterness of feeling on both sides of the Border. Foster wrote to Walsingham, saying, that he and the opposite warden had met for the redress of attempts committed on both sides, Russell being present to attend to particular causes of his own, "where it chanced a sudden accident and tumult to arise among the rascals of Scotland and England about a little pyckery among themselves, and we meaning no harm did sit the most of the day calling bills, and my Lord Russell among us. The said Lord Russell rose and went aside from us, with his own men, and there being in talk with a gentleman, was suddenly shot with a gun and slain in the midst of his own men, to the great discomfort of me and his poor friends in this country, and never a man either of England or Scotland but he. Alas! that the mischievous chance should happen for him to be killed with a shot, and none but him, which is the greatest discomfort that ever came upon me."

No hint is here given of any suspicion that Ker of Fernihurst was implicated in the death of this young man. Hence we are surprised to find that, on the day after this letter was written, Sir John Foster drew up a statement in which he gives an entirely different complexion to the incident. He asserts that it was not an accident. "Had it been an accident," he says, "or sudden breaking by rascals, as there was no such matter, the gentlemen of Scotland with their drums, fife, shot, and such as carried the 'ensigne' and 'penseller,' would have tarried with the warden; so that it appeareth plainly it was a 'pretended matter' beforehand, for the wardens sitting quietly calling their bills, the warden of England thinking no harm, the party of Scotland seeing the time serve for their 'former desire,' suddenly broke, striking up an alarm with sound of drum and fife, and gave the charge upon us—in which charge the Lord Russell was cruelly slain with shot, and so divers gentlemen of Scotland with their footmen and horsemen and whole force, followed and maintained their chase four miles within the Realm of England, and took sundry prisoners and horses, and carried them into Scotland, which they deny to deliver again."

This statement contradicts, in almost every particular, the asseverations deliberately made in the letter written the day before, and shows that even a gentleman in Sir John Foster's high position, with a deservedly great reputation for fair dealing, was capable, when occasion demanded, of twisting facts, or even inventing them, to suit his own ends, or the interest of the government he represented. It has been suggested that the English secretary, knowing that Fernihurst was an intimate friend of Arran, saw that by laying the blame of Lord Russell's death on the shoulders of the former, he might thereby procure the disgrace of this hated minister. Be this as it may, such conflicting assertions, made by the same person almost at the same time, should lead us to accept with a modified confidence other statements of a similar kind, as the spirit of party is no friend to the love of truth.

But despite the drawbacks and dangers attaching to such gatherings for the settlement of Border affairs, the day of truce was an institution of great public utility. It is difficult to see how, apart from such an arrangement, even the semblance of civilized life could have been maintained. The Borders really constituted an *imperium in imperio*, and the wardens, when presiding over their monthly convention, were to all intents and purposes absolute rulers within their own prescribed domain. It was generally found that when warden courts, or days of truce, were regularly held, good rule and order, at least judged by the ordinary Border standard, were well maintained throughout the entire district.

VII.

THE DEADLY FEUD.

"At the sacred font, the priest
Through ages left the master hand unblest
To urge with keener aim the blood incrusted spear."
  Leyden.

43

he difficulties with which the Borderers had to contend were of a varied character. They had to be constantly on the watch against the aggressions and incursions of their enemies on the opposite Marches. But it frequently happened that their most dangerous and inveterate foes were to be found amongst their own countrymen. This was the case more especially when blood-feuds arose, setting family against family, and clan against clan. An interesting, if not very luminous, account of the origin of the "Feud" is given by Burghley in a report submitted by him to the English government, in which he deals with what he calls the "Decays of the Borders." He says:—"Deadly Foed, the word of enmytie on the Borders, implacable without the blood and whole family destroyed, whose etymologie I know not where better to fetch than from Spiegelius in his *Lexicon Juris, in Verbo* 'feydum:' he saith it is an old Teutch word whereof is derived by Hermanus Nivoranus (?) *faydosum Hostis publicus*; 'foed' *enim, Bellum significat.*" He further points out that the Scottish wardens, being native Borderers, are "extraordinarilye adicted to parcialities, favour of their blood, tenantes and followers," and consequently he holds they should be disqualified for office.

The evils resulting from these deadly-feuds would have been comparatively trifling had it been possible to limit the consequences to the persons more immediately concerned. Owing, however, to the system of clanship which prevailed on the Borders, the whole sept became involved in the feud. "If one of the clan," says Sir Walter Scott, "chanced either to slay a man, or commit any similar aggression, the chief was expected to defend him by all means, legal or illegal. The most obvious and pacific was to pay such fine or *amende*, or assythement, as it was called, as might pacify the surviving relations, or make up the feud. This practice of receiving an atonement for slaughter seems also to have been part of the ancient Celtic usages; for it occurs in the Welch laws of Howell Dha, and was the very foundation of the Irish Brehon customs. The vestiges of it may be found in the common law of Scotland to this day. But poor as we have described the Border chief, and fierce as he certainly was by education and office, it was not often that he was either able or disposed to settle the quarrels of his clansmen in a manner so amicable and expensive. War was then resorted to; and it was the duty of the chief and clan who had sustained the injury to seek revenge by every means in their power, not only against the party who had given the offence, but, in the phrase of the time and country, against all his name, kindred, maintainers, and upholders. On the other hand, the chief and clan to whom the individual belonged who had done the offence, were equally bound in honour, by every means in their power, to protect their clansman, and to retaliate whatever injury the opposite party might inflict in their thirst of vengeance. When two clans were involved in this species of private warfare, which was usually carried on with the most ferocious animosity on both sides, they were said to be at deadly feud, and the custom is justly termed by the Scottish parliament most heathenish and barbarous.... In these deadly feuds, the chiefs of clans made war, or truce, or final peace with each other, with as much formality, and as little sincerity, as actual monarchs."

Feuds of the most bitter and hostile character were an every-day occurrence. The Herons, Fenwicks, Shafftownes, Charletons, and Milbornes, on the English side of the Border, were all at feud at the same time. And on the Scottish side the Elwoods (Elliots), Armstrongs, Nixons, Crosiers, Trumbles, and Olivers were, during the same period, at "daggers drawn," and thirsting for each other's blood. The misery which such feuds created can hardly be over-estimated. The sense of personal security was completely destroyed. Mutual trust, the primary condition of social life, was rendered practically impossible. And, as might be expected, the most trivial circumstances often gave rise to the most implacable hostility. A singular instance of this is referred to by John Cary in one of his communications to Burghley. He says:—"Your honour remembers hearing long since of the great road by the Scotts 'as Will Haskottes and his fellowes' made in Tynedale and Redesdale, taking up the whole country and nearly beggaring them for ever. On complaint to the Queen and Council, there was some redress made with much ado and many meetings. Buccleuch and the Scotts made some 'bragges and crackes' as that the country durst not take its own; but the Charletons being the 'sufficientest and ablest' men on the borders, not only took their own goods again, but encouraged their neighbours to do the like and not be afraid—'which hath ever since stuck in Buccleuch's stomack.'... Mary! he makes another quarrell, that long since in a war tyme, the Tynedale men should goe into his countrey, and there they took his grandfather and killed divers of his countrye, *and that they took away his grandfather's shworde*, and never let him have it yet synce. This sayeth he is the quarrell."

Nor did lapse of time tend to soften the animosities. The feud was inherited along with the rest of the family property. It was handed down from generation to generation. The son and grandson maintained it with a bitterness which, in some cases, seemed year by year to grow more intense. It affected more or less a man's whole social relationships, and gave rise to endless animosities and heart-burnings. Feuds were not unknown in other districts of the country, but owing to the feeble and ineffective manner in which the law was generally administered, they prevailed to a greater extent on the Borders,—and were characterised by a more vengeful spirit,—than in any other part of the kingdom.

Hence it was found that the existence of such feuds made the administration of the law, such as it was, a matter of supreme difficulty. It is said that it was hardly possible for any gentleman of the country to be of a jury of life and death if any of those at feud were indicted, "as they were grown so to seek blood that they would make a quarrel about the death of their grandfather, and kill any of the name." It was, therefore, found necessary to appoint special nobles and barons belonging to some distant part of the country, to sit in judgment in those cases in which the accused was at feud with the warden. On two occasions when courts were being held at Jedburgh, it was found expedient to issue proclamations in the King's name,—"That na maner of persons tak upon hand to invaid ane an uther for ald feid or new, now cumand to this present air or passand tharfra, and induring the tyme thairof under the pane of dede; and that na maner of persone or persons beir wapins except kniffis at their beltis, bot alanerlie our soverane lordis household, the justice, constable, merschell, compositouris, thair men and houshald, schireff, crounaris and thair deputis, under the pane of escheting of the wapins and punishing of the persons beraris therof." Owing to the disturbed condition of the country, such precautions were much needed, although it must be admitted that they did not always secure the end desired.

Many of the Border feuds present features of great interest alike to the sociologist and the historian. They afford interesting glimpses of the condition of society in this part of the realm, and disclose the dominant passions by which the lives and characters of those more immediately concerned were shaped and determined. Throughout the greater part of the 16th century a fierce feud raged between two of the most noted and powerful Border families—the Scotts and the Kers. The circumstances which gave rise to this deadly feud form an interesting chapter in the history of the Borders.

During the minority of James V. the Earl of Angus controlled the government of the country, and in his own interests, and for the furtherance of his own ends, kept a watchful eye on the movements of the young King. In the year 1525, James, accompanied by Angus, and other members of the court, came south to Jedburgh, "and held justice aires quhair manie plaintes cam to him of reiff, slauchter and oppression, bot little justice was used bot the purse, for thir was manie in that countrie war the Earl of Angus' kin and friendis, that got favourable justice, quhairof the king was not content, nor non of the rest of the lordis that war about him, for they wold have justice equally used to all men; bot the Earl of Angus and the rest of the Douglass' rulled yitt still as they pleased, and no man durst find fault with their proceidingis; quhairat the king was heartilie displeased, and would fain have been out of their handis, and for that effect he writt are secreitt letter to the laird of Buccleugh, desiring him effectuouslie that he wold come with all his forces, kin and freindis, and all that he might ax, and meit him at Melrose, at his home coming, and thair to tak him out of the Douglas' handis, and put him at libertie, to use himself among the rest of the lordis as he thought expedient." Buccleuch at once convened his "kin and freindis," and all who were prepared to take part with him, to the number of six hundred spears, and set out for Melrose to await the coming of the King. Home, Cessford, and Fernieherst, who were of the King's company, had returned home. Buccleuch and his followers made their appearance, arranged in order of battle, on Halidon Hill, overlooking the Tweed, near Melrose bridge. When Angus saw them he wondered what the hostile array portended. But when he discovered that Buccleuch was supported only by numbers of Annandale thieves, he took heart of grace, and said to the King—"Sir, yonder is the laird of Buccleuch, and the thieves of Annerdaill with him, to unbesett your grace in the way, bot I avow to God, Sir, they sall aither fight or flie. Thairfor, Sir, ye sall tarrie here, and my brither George with yow, and any other quhom yeu pleas, and I sall pas and put yon thieves aff the ground, and red the gaitt to your grace, or else die thairfor."

The conflict now began in earnest. Buccleuch and his men stoutly resisted the onslaught of Angus, and for a time the issue seemed uncertain. But Home, Cessford, and Fernieherst, having got wind of the affair, returned, supported by four score spears, "and sett on freschlie on the utmost wing, on the laird of Buccleughis field, and shortly bare them to the ground, quhilk caused the laird of Buccleugh to flie; on whom thair followed ane chaise be the lairdis of Sesfoord and Pherniherst, in the quhilk chaise the laird of Sesfoord was slain with ane cassin spear, be ane called Evan, servand of the laird of Buccleughis."

There seems nothing remarkable about such an incident as this. That Cessford should have been accidentally slain by one of Buccleuch's servants was no doubt a regrettable incident, but those who play bowls must be prepared for rubbers. This, unfortunately, was not the view entertained by the Kers, who henceforth were at deadly feud with Buccleuch. All efforts to bring about a reconciliation were in vain. The Kers thirsted for vengeance, and were determined to "bide their time." Twenty-six long years had come and gone, and one day as the laird of Buccleuch was passing along one of the streets of Edinburgh, little suspecting the fate which awaited him, he was fatally stabbed by the descendant of Cessford. The Borderers had many faults, but certainly they cannot be charged with having had short memories!

But a still more striking illustration of the disastrous consequences of the deadly feud is to be found in the case of the Johnstones and Maxwells, two of the most prominent and powerful families in Dumfriesshire. These two families were strong enough, had they been united, to have kept the whole district in good order; but unfortunately they were often at feud, with the result that not only their own interests, but the interests of the community as a whole, were ruthlessly sacrificed. It is worthy of note that one of the principal causes of the frequent and disastrous feuds between the representatives of the two families, was the frequency with which the office of warden was conferred, first on the one, and then on the other, without any good reason being assigned by the King for the adoption of this shuttle-cock policy. This office was naturally much coveted, as it was not only a source of revenue, which in those days was a most important consideration, but a condition of influence and power. It must, therefore, have been peculiarly irritating for the warden to be summarily called upon to resign his office almost before he had begun to reap the rewards pertaining to it. And when he saw his rival basking in the sunshine of the royal favour, from which he had been suddenly and capriciously excluded, his feelings may be more easily imagined than described. Nor did it greatly tend to soothe his wounded feelings to reflect that the person by whom he had been superseded would be certain before long to be hurled from his proud eminence and another put in his place. The whole system was pernicious, and was the source of no end of mischief and bad blood.

The origin of this famous feud may be briefly related. John, seventh Lord Maxwell, has been well described as one of those men whom a daring and restless temperament and their crimes "have damned to eternal fame." After the death of the Regent Morton, he succeeded in securing a charter to the Earldom of Morton—his mother, Lady Beatrix Douglas, being the Regent's second daughter. It was not his good fortune, however, to enjoy for a lengthened period either the title, or the domains attached to it. In January, 1585, four years after he had come into possession, Parliament rescinded the Attainder, and declared that the title and the estates were to be conferred on the Regent Morton's lawful heir. Maxwell was declared a rebel, mainly owing to his religious views—he being a warm adherent of the Romish Church—and Johnstone was commissioned to apprehend him. Though he had the assistance of two bands of hired soldiers, Maxwell proved more than a match for him, took him prisoner, and set fire to Lochwood Castle, as it was savagely remarked, "that Lady Johnstone might have light to put on her hood." This unexpected blow fell on the laird of Johnstone with crushing effect. In the following year he died of a broken heart. It is to these circumstances that we must attribute the origin of the deadly feud between the two clans, and especially between their chiefs.

But Maxwell, though gaining this important victory, was not allowed to escape. He was ultimately taken prisoner, but afterwards regained his liberty, on condition that he left the country. He went to Spain, and offered his services to "His Catholic Majesty," who was then busily engaged in fitting out the *Invincible Armada*, by which he hoped to overwhelm both England and Scotland. Lord Maxwell—so little was he animated by the spirit of patriotism—entered into the scheme *con amore*. Being furnished with ample means, he returned to Scotland in 1588 to levy men on the Borders to assist his new sovereign. His prefidious designs were fortunately discovered, and ere he could make good his escape, he was surprised by the King in Dumfries, taken prisoner, and his wardenship of the West Marches bestowed on his powerful rival, the laird of Johnstone. Everything might have gone on smoothly at this juncture had the King only been gifted with a little firmness and foresight. He was anxious, however, to conciliate his Roman Catholic subjects, and he seems to have come to the conclusion that, reasonable conditions being imposed, he might accomplish this end by restoring Maxwell to favour and office. This was a fatal blunder, and produced disastrous results. Though the two rival chiefs were induced to enter into a bond of alliance to support each other in their lawful quarrels, as might have been expected, it was not long before circumstances arose which brought them again into deadly conflict. The Johnstones seemed to have concluded that they were at liberty to harry and despoil at their pleasure, so long as they left unmolested any of the name of Maxwell. Acting upon this principle, they made a raid upon Nithsdale, and committed sundry depredations on Lord Sanquhar, the lairds of Drumlanrig, Closeburn, and Lagg, and killed eighteen persons who had "followed their own goods." Such a fierce and unprovoked assault could not well be allowed to go unpunished, and so a commission was given to Lord Maxwell to pursue the Johnstones with all hostilities. Johnstone hearing of this, at once adopted measures for his protection.

He summoned to his aid the Scotts of Teviotdale, and the Grahams and Elliots of Eskdale, as well as "divers Englishmen, treasonably brought within the realm, armed in plain hostility." Maxwell, however, determined not to be beat, entered into "Bonds of Manrent" with Sanquhar, Drumlanrig, and several others, who had suffered at the hands of Johnstone, to maintain each other's quarrels.

Acting upon his commission, Maxwell summoned Johnstone to surrender, but this he refused to do, on the ground that the warden had acted illegally in entering into "Bonds" with the persons above-mentioned. As it was clearly impossible to settle the question by diplomatic means, the warden despatched Captain Oliphant with some troops to Lochmaben, to await his arrival in Annandale. The Johnstones, who were on the alert, coming suddenly upon them, killed the captain, and a number of his soldiers, and burned the Kirk of Lochmaben, where some of Oliphant's men had fled for refuge. Lord Maxwell now entered the field in person. He expected to raise the different towns in his aid; but Johnstone, acting on the principle that "a 'steek' in time saves nine," attacked him at once, scattered his forces, and slew Lord Maxwell, "and sundry gentlemen of his name." This affair took place December, 1593, and is well known as the Battle of Dryfe Sands. "Lord Maxwell," it is said, "a tall man, and heavy in armour, was in the chase overtaken and stricken from his horse. The report went that he called to Johnstone, and desired to be taken (prisoner), as he had formerly taken his (Johnstone's) father: but was unmercifully used; and the hand that reached forth cut off; but of this I can affirm nothing. There, at all events, the Lord Maxwell fell, having received many wounds. He was a nobleman of great spirit, humane, courteous, and more learned than noblemen commonly are; but aspiring and ambitious of rule."

In this contest the Maxwells suffered severely. They were cut down in scores in the streets of Lockerbie. It is said that those who escaped bore on them to their dying hour marks of the fatal day, which occasioned the proverbial phrase of "a Lockerby lick," to denote a frightful gash over the face or skull. So dreadful was the carnage in this disastrous "bout of arms" that it is alleged by numerous historians that at least 700 of the Maxwells and their adherents were slain. Two aged thorns long marked the spot where Maxwell met his fate, known in the district as "Maxwell's Thorns." They were carried away by a flood some fifty years ago, but have been replaced by two others, now enclosed in a railing.

"It is evident, then," remarks Pitcairn, "according to the sentiments of those times, inherited from their earliest years, which 'grew with their growth and strengthened with their strength,' that natural duty and filial piety required such a feud should become hereditary, and behoved should be handed down from one generation to another. The attempts by the King and his Council to procure an effectual reconciliation, although strenuously made and often repeated, at length proved abortive. The re-appointment of the Laird of Johnstone to be warden of the West Marches, in 1596, appears to have served as a signal for the resumption of mutual aggressions." It would seem that Johnstone held the office at this time for a period of three years, but as his wardenry had got into a most unsatisfactory condition, he was superseded by Sir John Carmichael, his appointment being notified to Lord Scrope, by James VI., on the 26th December, 1599. Carmichael was murdered by Thomas Armstrong, "son of Sandies Ringan," in the following year, and Johnstone was again appointed to this ill-fated office. All this time the feud raged as fiercely as ever. Various attempts were made to bring about an agreement, but nothing came of them. At length through the influence of mutual friends, a private meeting was arranged. Solemn pledges were given and exchanged, and Lord Maxwell and Sir James Johnstone met on the 6th of April, 1608, each accompanied only by a single attendant. The principals having removed some distance to discuss their affairs, a quarrel arose between the two attendants, and when Sir James Johnstone turned round to admonish them to keep the peace, Lord Maxwell suddenly drew his pistol, and fired at him, and shot him through the back with two bullets.

This cold-blooded murder, made all the more heinous by the circumstances in which it was perpetrated, was amply revenged. Lord Maxwell was apprehended, and put in ward in the Castle of Edinburgh. He contrived, however, to escape, and went abroad, where he remained for four years. He returned to the Borders, but finding that his crime was remembered against him, had instantly to prepare for embarkation to Sweden. Unfortunately for himself, he was persuaded by his kinsman, the Earl of Caithness, to abandon this project. He was lured to Castle Sinclair, where he was promised shelter and secrecy. He was not long there before he was betrayed by his friend, taken prisoner, and brought to Edinburgh and beheaded. "It may be gratifying to know that the Earl of Caithness obtained no reward for his traitorous conduct; but, on the contrary, his treachery served as a source of constant reproach to him and his family."

"Thus was finally ended, by a salutary example of severity, 'the foul debate' betwixt the Maxwells and the Johnstones, in course of which each family lost two chieftains; one by dying of a broken heart, one in the field of battle, one by assassination, and one by the sword of the executioner."

The history of the Borders unfortunately affords too many examples of the deplorable consequences arising from the prevalency and frequency of such feuds. Many were compelled to live in constant terror of the dagger of the assassin, never knowing the moment when they might be stricken down by an unseen hand. At the same time it may be remarked that those who were guilty of the crime of murder found it a matter of extreme difficulty to escape punishment. The "avenger of blood" was ever on the track, and though for a time, by means of various disguises, the culprit might elude pursuit, he had sooner or later to pay the penalty of his misdeeds.

In the year 1511 Sir Robert Ker of Cessford was slain at a Border meeting by three Englishmen—Heron, Starhead, and Lillburn. The English monarch delivered up Lillburn to justice, but the other two made good their escape. Starhead fled for refuge to the very centre of England, and there lived in secrecy and upon his guard. Two dependants of the murdered warden were deputed by Andrew Ker of Cessford to revenge his father's death. They travelled through England in various disguises till they discovered the place of Starhead's retreat, murdered him in his bed, and brought his head to their master, by whom, in memorial of their vengeance, it was exposed on the cross of Edinburgh. Heron would have shared the same fate had he not spread abroad a report of his having died of the plague, and caused his funeral obsequies to be performed.

Various expedients were resorted to in order to terminate the feuds which prevailed. A common method was to get the Chiefs and Chieftains of the opposing clans to subscribe what were called "bonds of assurance." There can be no doubt that this might often have proved a most effective measure, had the parties concerned only been willing to let bygones be bygones. But it was found that the old sores were not easily healed. Despite the utmost precautions, animosities which had been suppressed for a time—kept as it were in abeyance—would assert themselves in a most unexpected manner, and with redoubled force, and create a still more distracting condition of affairs.

Prior to the Reformation, feuds were sometimes terminated by an appeal to the religious sensibilities of the persons more immediately concerned. They were induced to make pilgrimages to noted shrines—the shrine of St. Ninian being a favourite resort—where, under the influence of religious thoughts and feelings, they might be induced to take a more kindly view of those with whom they were at feud, and make some reparation for the injury they had inflicted. How far this method succeeded it is difficult to determine, but the likelihood is that it was quite as effective as any other.

Among the Chiefs, or clans, feuds were sometimes brought to an end by a contract of marriage between a leading gentleman of one clan and a daughter of the principal house of the other. This was the plan adopted by the Scotts and Kers, and which, after some vexatious delays, proved entirely successful.

But if it was found that none of the above methods of terminating the feud could be conveniently applied, then resort was had, as has already been hinted, to still simpler means. An atonement was made by the payment of a sum of money called "assythment," which was sometimes found sufficient to restore good feeling, and bring together in a spirit of amity families that had been at feud with each other.

But these and other means of putting an end to the feud proved, perhaps, in the majority of cases, of little or no avail. The parties concerned preferred, generally, to fight it out to the bitter end, utterly indifferent to consequences.

VIII.

THE THIEVES DAUNTONED.

"Revenge! revenge! auld Wat 'gan cry;
Fye, lads, lay on them cruellie!
We'll ne'er see Teviotside again,
Or Willie's death revenged sall be."

The intermittent and ineffective manner in which the law was generally administered on the Borders was the occasion, if not the cause, of much of the turbulence and lawlessness which prevailed. The Border thieves were now and then placed under the most rigid surveillance, and their misdeeds visited with condign punishment; but for the most part they were left to work out their own sweet will, none daring to make them afraid.

This method of treatment could not be expected to produce beneficial results. It had exactly the opposite effect. Respect for the law was completely destroyed. Those who were called upon, as the phrase goes, "to underlie the law," had no sense of shame when their wrongdoing was brought home to them. They no doubt felt the inconvenience of being punished, by fine or imprisonment, for their misdeeds; but there was no moral stigma attaching to imprisonment, or to almost any other form of punishment. That a man's father had been hanged for cattle-stealing, or for the slaughter of those who had dared to resist him when he went on a foraging expedition, might engender a feeling of resentment, but it was not in the least likely to create a feeling of shame. Such incidents as these were regarded with philosophical indifference. We remember once hearing a distinguished Borderer remark that the ancient history of nearly all the great Border families had been faithfully chronicled in "Pitcairn's Criminal Trials!" A careful study of that interesting and valuable compilation will go far to corroborate the remark. The "Family Tree" is a phrase which has an altogether peculiar significance on the Borders. It suggests ideas and reflections which are not usually associated with genealogy.

But when all has been said on this phase of the question which either envy or malice can suggest, every sympathetic and well-informed student of Border history will readily admit that the Borderers, bad as they were, were really more sinned against than sinning. Carlyle has somewhere remarked that a man's first *right* is to be well governed. It is, perhaps, unusual to regard our rights from this point of view, yet there can be no doubt that good government is an essential requisite of society, and one of the greatest blessings of the individual life. This boon was one which, for many generations, the Borderers did not enjoy. They were encouraged to commit crime one day, and punished for it the next. This is doubtless a strong assertion, but we think it is one that can be amply proved. It was the policy of James VI., for example, to keep on the best possible terms with Queen Elizabeth, in order not to endanger his chance of succession, and consequently he was naturally anxious to keep his turbulent subjects on the Borders as well in hand as possible. But that he secretly sympathised with them, and encouraged them in their predatory incursions on the English Border, hardly admits of serious doubt. Sir John Foster, writing in 1586, says: "The King doth write to the Laird of Cessford to do justice, and yet in the meantime he appointeth others to ride and break the Border, and doth wink thereat." We find Hunsdon writing in the same strain. "I am at this present credibly advertised," he says, "from one of good intelligence that what fair weather soever the King makes, he means no good towards her Majesty, nor her subjects, and that at this present, there is some practice in hand, whatsoever it is—and he doth assure me that those of Liddesdale, Ewesdale, Eskdale, and Annandale, being 400 horse that came to Hawden brigges where they took away the goods and burnt 4 houses, was not without the King's knowledge, but not meant to be done in that place." In another communication, in which he alludes to the coming of the King to the Borders with a large army, ostensibly to punish the thieves, he remarks, that he thought it very strange that the King should come with so great a company for the suppressing of a few thieves, when there was not one of them, either in Liddesdale or Teviotdale, that he might not have had brought to him, had he so wished it. He hints that these great outrages would never have been attempted without the King's "privitie"—"for it was given forth," he says, "that the Earl Bothwell's riding to Branksome and Hawick, where he holds as many of Liddesdale before him as it pleased him to send for, that it was to cause them of Liddesdale to be answerable to justice to England for such outrages as they had sundry times committed; but the sequel did manifest the cause of his going thither. For presently after, his said son-in-law, the Laird of Buccleuch, made a 'roade' with 300 horse into the West March at two of the clock in the after-noon, with a trumpet and gydon, and spoiled the country about Bewcastle in warlike manner till sun-set. The trumpet was my Lord Bothwell's, and the goods was carried to Armitage at my Lord Bothwell's officers' commandment. So as I have just cause to think that this 'roade' was done by my Lord Bothwell's appointment, and I am sure he durst not have done it without the King's privity, I will not say commandment."

These are only a few of many illustrations of a similar kind which may be found scattered through the pages of the "State Papers," and while we must be careful not to accept such statements as in every instance worthy of absolute credence, yet the circumstances would seem to warrant our regarding them, in many cases at least, as well founded. When the King and his lieutenants thus secretly connived at, and encouraged, the depredations of the reivers, we need hardly wonder that they engaged in the work of plundering with an almost total absence of compunction.

Had the sphere of their operations been always strictly confined to the English Border, the likelihood is that neither King, nor Regent, would have sought to "daunton" them. But there were times when it was difficult for the Scottish reivers to earn a decent livelihood by harassing and spoiling "the auld enemy," owing to the watchfulness and strength of those dwelling within the opposite Marches; and as there was a danger of their talents becoming feeble through disuse, they naturally turned their attention to their own more wealthy neighbours and friends. That there is "honour among thieves" is a proposition that is sometimes called in question; but we find that the spirit of a really helpful friendship occasionally manifested itself in curious ways. When a family, or clan, contemplated a raid upon a neighbour's property, it was customary to secure the assistance of the thieves on the opposite Border. In "Pitcairn's Criminal Trials" there are numerous allusions to the prosecutions of famous Scottish reivers for the inbringing of Englishmen to assist them in the work of plunder. This was one of the offences charged against Cockburn of Henderland, and which, no doubt, weighed heavily with his judges in consigning him to the gallows.

When the reivers thus turned their attention to their own countrymen, and with the assistance of English allies began to despoil them, it was felt that strong measures must be adopted for their suppression and punishment. The Border reivers regarded the law with a feeling akin to contempt. They were disposed to look upon the statutes of the realm as so many old wives' fables; and, truth to speak, they were often of not much more account. The policy of the wardens was too frequently one of mere self-aggrandizement, and so long as their individual interests were not imperilled they looked on with a kind of placid indifference at the misdoings of those whom it was their duty, if not their interest, to control. When James VI. came to Dumfries, to "daunton the thieves" in that district of the country, his time was mainly occupied in meting out summary punishment to men of high social position, whose "thefts, herschips, and slaughters" had become notorious, and cried aloud for vengeance. There were, no doubt, many of the commonality as well, who at this time were made to suffer for their crimes, but as these cases were generally dealt with by subordinate officials, they do not come so prominently before us. "Nothing is more remarkable," says Sir Herbert Maxwell, "than the light thrown on the social state of Scotland at this time by the justiciary records. By far the larger part of the criminals dealt with at the King's 'justice aires' were men of good position, barons and landowners, burgesses or provosts of burghs. The humbler offenders were dealt with by the sheriff or at the baron's courts, and do not appear; but the following extracts from the records of the short reign of James IV., in which the culprits are all landowners, or members of their families, in Dumfriesshire or Galloway, illustrate the difficulty of maintaining order when the upper classes were so unruly." Here a list of names is appended, in which such well-known personages as Murray, Jardine, Herries, Bell, Dinwoodie, Lindsay, Douglas, &c., appear. These men stand charged with high treason, forethought—felony, slaughter, horse-stealing, and other heinous offences. Some were pardoned, others respited, the horse-stealer was called upon to make restitution,—a severe sentence,—and Lindsay of Wauchope, who had slain a messenger-at-arms, was condemned to death, and his estates forfeited. In the accounts of expenditure incurred by the King during this visit to Dumfries some curious items appear. Here are a few samples. *Item*, to the man that hangit the thieves at the Hallirlaws,—xiiijs. *Item*, for ane raip to hang them in ...—viijd. *Item*, to the man that hangit the thieves in Canonby, be the King's command ...—xiiijs. But all the details are not of this gruesome character. The work of hanging, needful as it was, could give but "sma' pleasure" even to a King, and so we find that entertainment of another kind was plentifully provided for the youthful monarch. "He was attended in his progress," says Tytler, "by his huntsmen, falconers, morris dancers, and all the motley and various minions of his pleasure, as well as by his judges and ministers of the law; and whilst troops of the unfortunate marauders were seized and brought in irons to the encampment, executions and entertainments appear to have succeeded each other with extraordinary rapidity."

Not long after the King made another visit to the Borders, coming on this occasion also with a considerable following, to the Water of Rule, to "daunton" the Turnbulls, whose excesses had filled the minds of the more peaceful inhabitants with a feeling of terror. Leslie, in his own quaint and picturesque style, thus describes the incident:—"The King raid furth of Edinburgh, the viij. of November one the nycht, weill accumpaneit to the watter of Roulle, quhair he tuik divers brokin men and brocht thame to Jeduart; of quhom sum was justifyeit, and the principallis of the trubillis come in lyning claythis, with nakitt sordis in thair handis and wyddyis about thair neckis, and pat thame in the Kingis will; quha wes send to divers castells in ward, with sindrie utheris of that cuntrey men also, quhair throchout the bordouris wes in greiter quietnes thairefter."

We find that the Regents, when occasion demanded, were no less severe in their treatment of the unfortunate marauders. It would seem that about the middle of the sixteenth century the Borders had attained to an almost unexampled degree of lawlessness. Murder, robbery, and offences of all kinds prevailed to an intolerable extent. It is said that men who had been publicly outlawed walked abroad, deriding the terrors of justice. Hawick, a burgh of ancient renown, was the centre of these crimes. The Earl of Mar made a sudden and rapid march upon the town, encompassed it with his soldiers, and made a proclamation in the market place forbidding any one, on pain of death, to receive or shelter a thief. He apprehended fifty-three of the most noted outlaws, eighteen of whom, strange to state, he was under the necessity of drowning for "lack of trees and halters." Six were hanged in Edinburgh, and the rest either acquitted or put in prison. This sharp and salutary lesson was evidently laid to heart, as we learn that, for some time after, extraordinary quietness prevailed.

In a few years, however, the state of matters on the Borders seems to have gone from bad to worse. The Scotts and the Ellwoods (Elliots) were at deadly feud, and as the result of their frequent and violent quarrels the whole district was thrown into confusion and disorder. Queen Mary had recently returned from France; and, hearing how things were going in this distracted part of her realm, came to Jedburgh to hold court in person. For more than a week she was busily engaged in hearing a great variety of cases that were brought before her, and imposing various modes and degrees of punishment on the offenders. It was on this occasion she made her famous visit to Hermitage Castle, in Liddesdale. The Earl of Bothwell had been stationed there for some time, in order if possible to "daunton" the "wicked limmers" by whom the district had long been infested. One day when in pursuit of a party of Elliots, having got considerably ahead of his company, he encountered a famous mosstrooper, John Elliot of Park, the "little Jock Elliot" of Border song (?), and drawing a "dag" or pistol fired at him, wounding him severely in the thigh. The gallant marauder turned upon his assailant, and, with a two-handed sword, which he wielded with amazing dexterity, bore him to the ground, leaving him to all appearance dead. Some have been wicked enough to wish that this *coup d'epée* had been more effective, as both Queen and country would have been spared much trouble and many heart burnings had Elliot's well-aimed blow fallen with more deadly effect. Mary, hearing that her favourite courtier lay ill at Hermitage, resolved to pay him a friendly visit. Leaving Jedburgh early in the morning, in the company of her brother Murray, and other officers, she rode by way of Hawick over the hills to Liddesdale—a distance of twenty miles. The road was rough, and not without its hazards, especially to one unacquainted with the district—the ground near the watershed being full of quaking bogs and treacherous morasses. There is a place still known as the "Queen's Mire," near the head of the Braidlie burn, where the palfrey on which her Majesty was riding came to grief. Not long ago a bit of a silver spur was found at this spot, which is not unreasonably regarded as a relic of the Queen's disaster.

After watching by the bed of the sufferer for the space of two hours, the Queen resumed her journey, reaching Jedburgh the same night. This long and exciting ride, which has exposed the memory of the fair Queen to many severe animadversions, was followed by a violent fever, which brought her to the gates of death. She herself did not expect to recover. Calling her nobles around her couch she enjoined them to live in unity and peace with each other, and to employ their utmost diligence in the government of the country, and the education of her son. But the end was not yet. Fotheringay, with its tragic memories, and not the quiet Border town where she then lay, was to witness the close of her sublimely pathetic career.

The unsettled condition of the country after the battle of Langside, and the Queen's flight into England, made the Border reivers more than ever bold and lawless. They seemed to think that their opportunity had come, and that they might shake themselves free from the embarrassing restraints of constituted authority. But they were speedily made to feel that the hand of the Regent was even heavier than that of the King. The Earl of Murray, realizing that repressive measures were urgently needed, mustered a force of 4000 horse and foot and marched into Teviotdale, where he was speedily joined by Scott of Buccleuch, Home, Ker of Cessford, Ker of Ferniherst, and other gentlemen. After consulting together it was resolved to burn and destroy Liddesdale; and Buccleuch and Ferniherst were deputed to undertake the work. This resolution, as might have been expected, created consternation and dismay amongst the leaders of the clans, who came to the Regent entreating him to stay his hand, and graciously pardon their offences. Murray was not unwilling to do so, provided they would give assurances and pledges of their future conduct.

It was found impossible, however, to come to terms. The sureties offered did not satisfy the Regent, and he at once set about the wholesale work of destruction which he had formerly planned. He was determined to do the work thoroughly when he had begun. Everything that would burn was given to the flames. Not a single house was left standing. He spent a Sunday night in the castle of Mangerton, and when he left next morning he had the satisfaction of seeing it reduced to a heap of ruins. This destructive invasion must have taxed the energies of his large army, as it is said that the Armstrongs and Elliots had fifty keeps and castles on the banks of the Liddle. It is one thing, however, to destroy the rookeries; it is another and totally different thing to exterminate the crows. The Border thieves were not difficult to accommodate. They were inured to hardship. It was a necessity of their mode of life. Their "peels" and "towers" might be in ruins, but it never seemed to have occurred to them to go elsewhere, at least for any length of time. As soon as the avenging army had withdrawn, they were back to their old haunts, and in a short time had them as comfortable as ever. When a community has been demoralized by long continued misgovernment, the mere application of brute force does not go far in the way of restraining them, or helping them toward a better mode of life—a lesson which governments are often slow to learn.

But this work of "dauntoning the thieves" was also occasionally undertaken by the wardens with considerable heartiness, more especially when dealing with unfortunate culprits from the opposite wardenry. Sir Robert Cary frequently distinguished himself in this way. In his chatty and interesting "Memoirs," he tells a story of one *Geordie Bourne*, whom he caused to be hanged on account of his villainies. It is to be hoped that the picture he has drawn of this man is not representative of the reivers as a whole, as it is hardly possible to conceive of a more consummate scoundrel. We shall let the warden tell the story in his own words. He says:—"This gallant with some of his associates, would, in a bravery, come and take goods in the East March. I had that night some of the garrison abroad. They met with this Geordie and his fellows driving off cattle before them. The garrison set upon them, and with a shot killed Geordie Bourne's uncle, and he himself bravely resisting, till he was sore hurt in the head, was taken. After he was taken, his pride was such as he asked who it was that durst avow that night's work? But when he heard it was the garrison, he was then more quiet. But so powerful and awful was this Sir Robert Car and his favourites, as there was not a gentleman in the East March that durst offend them. Presently, after he was taken, I had most of the gentlemen of the March come to me, and told me that now I had the ball at my foot, and might bring Sir Robert Car to what condition I pleased; for this man's life was so near and dear to him, as I should have all that heart could desire for the good and quiet of the country and myself, if upon any condition I would give him his life. I heard them and their reasons; notwithstanding, I called a jury the next morning, and he was found guilty of March treason. Then they feared that I would cause him to be executed that afternoon, which made them come flocking to me that I should spare his life till the next day; and if Sir Robert Car came not himself to me, and made me not such proffers as I could not but accept, then I should do with him what I pleased. And, further, they told me plainly that if I should execute him before I heard from Sir Robert Car, they must be forced to quit their houses and fly the country; for his fury would be such against me and the March I commanded, as he would use all his power and strength to the utter destruction of the East March. They were so earnest with me, that I gave them my word he should not die that day. There was post upon post sent to Sir Robert Car; and some of them rode to him themselves to advertise him in what danger Geordie Bourne was; how he was condemned, and should have been executed that afternoon, but, by their humble suit, I gave them my word that he should not die that day; and therefore besought him that he would send to me with all speed he could, to let me know that he would be next day with me to offer good conditions for the safety of his life. When all things were quiet and the watch set at night, after supper, about ten of the clock, I took one of my men's liveries and put it about me, and took two other of my servants with me in their liveries, and we three, as the warden's men, came to the Provost Marshal's, where Bourne was, and were let into his chamber. We sat down by him, and told him that we were desirous to see him, because we heard he was stout and valiant and true to his friend; and that we were sorry our master could not be moved to spare his life. He voluntarily of himself said that he had lived long enough to do so many villainies as he had done, and withal told us that he had lain with above forty men's wives, what in England, what in Scotland; and that he had killed seven Englishmen with his own hand, cruelly murdering them; that he had spent his whole time in whoring, drinking, stealing, and taking deep revenge for slight offences. He seemed to be very penitent, and much desired a minister for the comfort of his soul. We promised him to let our master know his desire, who, we knew, would presently grant it. We took our leave of him, and presently I took order that Mr Selby, a very worthy honest preacher, should go to him, and not stir from him till his execution the next morning; for after I had heard his own confession, I was resolved no conditions should save his life; and so took order that, at the gate's opening next morning, he should be carried to execution, which accordingly was performed."

Milder measures were sometimes adopted, and proved surprisingly efficacious—in certain circumstances. Before Sir Robert Cary was warden of the East March he was deputy to Lord Scrope, his brother-in-law, who was warden of the West March, with his headquarters in Carlisle. On one occasion, when occupying this subordinate position, intelligence was brought to him that two Scotsmen had killed a churchman in Scotland, and that they had been relieved or sheltered by one of the Græmes of Netherby. Cary determined to surprise the fugitive Scots, and about two o'clock one morning surrounded the Tower of Netherby with twenty-five horsemen. As he approached he saw a boy riding from the house as fast as his horse could carry him. Thomas Carelton came to him and said, "Do you see that boy that rideth away as fast? He will be in Scotland within this half hour, and he is gone to let them know that you are here, and the small number you have with you; and that if they make haste, on a sudden they may surprise us, and do with us what they please." But Cary was not to be frightened. He soon gathered together three or four hundred horse from the surrounding district and as many foot, and presently set to work to get to the top of the strong tower into which the Scots had fled for refuge. The Scots, seeing how things were going, pled for mercy. "They had no sooner opened the iron gate," says Cary, "and yielded themselves my prisoners, but we might see four hundred horse within a quarter of a mile coming to their rescue, and to surprise me and my small company; but of a sudden they stayed, and stood at gaze. Then had I more to do than ever, for all our Borderers came crying with full mouths, 'Sir, give us leave to set upon them, for these are they that have killed our fathers, our brothers, our uncles, and our cousins; and they are come, thinking to surprise you, upon weak grass nags, such as they could get on a sudden; and God will put them into your hands, that we may take revenge of them for much blood that they have spilled of ours.' I desired that they would be patient and wise, and bethought myself, if I should give them their wills, there should be few or none of them (the Scots) that would escape unkilled (there were so many deadly feuds among them), and therefore I resolved with myself to give a fair answer, but not to give them their desire. So I told them that if I were not there myself, they might do what pleased themselves; but being present, if I should give them leave, the blood that had been spilt that day would lie very heavy on my conscience, and therefore I desired them, for my sake, to forbear; and if the Scots did not presently make away with all the speed they could upon my sending to them, they should then have their wills to do what they pleased. They were ill satisfied with my answer, but durst not disobey. I sent with speed to the Scots, and bade them pack away with all the speed they could, for if they stayed the messengers' return, there should few of them return to their own home. They made no stay, but they were turned homewards before the messenger had made an end of his message. Thus, by God's mercy and by my means, there were a great many lives spared that day."

Thus ended happily what might otherwise have proved a disastrous encounter. Such incidents tend to prove that the Borderers might have been governed with comparative ease had they only been dealt with in a firm but kindly spirit. The rough usage to which they were frequently subjected at the hands of the government made them reckless, and not unnaturally led them to regard the law not as a friend, but as an enemy.

IX.

LIDDESDALE LIMMERS.

"Wicked thieves and limmers."

Act of Parliament.

"Thir limmer thieves, they have good hearts,
They nevir think to be o'erthrown;
Three banners against Weardale men they bare,
As if the world had been their own."

Rookhope Ryde.

Though reiving may be said to have been a characteristic of the inhabitants along the whole Border line from Berwick to the Solway, yet it was only in the district known as Liddesdale where it attained, what we might designate, its complete development as a thoroughly organized system. This part of Roxburghshire is, to a certain extent, detached from the rest of the county by reason of the fact that it lies south of the range of hills which form the watershed between the Solway and the German Ocean. This picturesque and interesting district, so famous in Border song and story, is of a somewhat triangular shape, and at present forms one of the largest parishes in the south of Scotland, measuring some twenty miles by fourteen. It is bounded by England on the south, by Dumfriesshire on the west, and by the parishes of Teviothead, Hobkirk, and Southdean on the north. The upper, or northern, portion is mountainous and bleak. Some of the hills along its boundaries are high and precipitous, the lofty peaks of Millenwood Fell and Windhead attaining an elevation of close on 2000 feet. Tudhope hill, which forms a landmark for ships at sea, is 1830 feet high. The lower end of the district is less mountainous, but the whole country is wild and bare, except in the valleys, which are clothed in the richest green, and are sunny and sheltered.

Along the banks of the Hermitage and the Liddle—the latter stream giving its name to the district—the keeps and peels of the Border reivers were thickly and picturesquely planted. These towers, many of which have been happily preserved, form one of the most striking features of the Border landscape. As a general rule they were built in some situation of great natural strength, on a precipice, or close to the banks of a stream, or surrounded by woods and morasses, which made them difficult of access. The position in which they were generally placed indicated at a glance the pursuits and apprehensions of their inhabitants. It is said that when James VI. approached the castle of Lochwood, the ancient seat of the Johnstones, he exclaimed that "the man who built it must have been a knave in his heart."

The principal part of these strongholds consisted of a large square tower, called a "keep," having walls of immense thickness, which could be easily defended against any sudden or desultory assault. The residencies of the inferior Chiefs, called "peels" or "bastel-houses," were generally built on a much smaller scale, and consisted merely of a high square tower, surrounded by an outer wall, which served as a protection for cattle at night. In these places the rooms were placed, one above the other, and connected by a narrow stair, which was easily blocked up or defended, so that it was possible for the garrison to hold out for a considerable period, even after the lower storey had been taken possession of by the enemy. In such circumstances the usual device was for the assailants to heap together quantities of wetted straw, and set fire to it in order to drive the defenders from storey to storey, and thus compel them to surrender.

"In each village or town," says Sir Walter Scott, "were several small towers having battlements projecting over the side walls, and usually an advanced angle or two, with shot-holes for flanking the doorway, which was always defended by a strong door of oak, studded with nails, and often by an interior door of iron. These small peel-houses were ordinarily inhabited by the principal feuars and their families. Upon the alarm of approaching danger, the whole inhabitants thronged from their miserable cottages, which were situated around, to garrison these places of defence. It was then no easy matter for an hostile party to penetrate into the village, for the men were habituated to the use of bow and fire-arms; and the towers being generally so placed that the discharge from one crossed that from another, it was impossible to assault any of them individually."

In the middle of the sixteenth century there were no fewer than sixteen of these bastel-houses in the village of Lessudden, a fact which shows that the inhabitants of the Border were compelled to live under somewhat peculiar conditions. To follow the ordinary occupations of life was, in most cases, all but impossible.

One of the most important strongholds on the Borders was Hermitage, a well-built castle, placed near the watershed, on the banks of a swift-flowing mountain stream—the Hermitage water, which joins the Liddle a little above the village of Newcastleton. This famous Border tower was built and fortified by Walter, Earl of Menteith, in the beginning of the thirteenth century. It was a royal fortress, built and maintained for the defence of the Kingdom. Numerous interesting associations cluster around its mouldering walls. It has, unhappily, been the scene of many a blood-curdling tragedy. Could its massive walls only recount the deeds which have been done under their shadow, they would many a strange tale unfold. Hermitage was long associated with the name of Lord Soulis, a fiend in human form, whose crimes have been painted in blackest hues, and to whom tradition has ascribed almost every conceivable kind and degree of wickedness. He seems, at least, to have been utterly destitute of the divine quality of mercy.

"The axe he bears, it hacks and tears;
'Tis form'd of an earth-fast flint;
No armour of knight, tho' ever so wight,
Can bear its deadly dint.

No danger he fears, for a charm'd sword he wears,
Of adderstone the hilt;
No Tynedale knight had ever such might,
But his heart-blood was spilt."

He invited the young laird of Mangerton to a feast, and treacherously murdered him. The "Cout of Keeldar," also, was drowned by the retainers of Lord Soulis in a pool near the castle, being held down in the water by the spears of his murderers.

"And now young Keeldar reach'd the stream,
Above the foamy linn;
The Border lances round him gleam,
And force the warrior in.

The holly floated to the side,
And the leaf on the rowan pale;
Alas! no spell could charm the tide,
Nor the lance of Liddesdale.

Swift was the Cout o' Keeldar's course
Along the lily lee;
But home came never hound nor horse,
And never home came he.

Where weeps the birch with branches green,
Without the holy ground,
Between two old gray stones is seen
The warrior's ridgy mound.

And the hunters bold, of Keeldar's train,
Within yon castle's wall,
In a deadly sleep must aye remain,

Till the ruin'd towers down fall.

Each in his hunter's garb array'd,
Each holds his bugle horn;
Their keen hounds at their feet are laid
That ne'er shall wake the morn."

Tradition says that, when the people complained to the King of the atrocities committed by Lord Soulis, he said to them in a fit of irritation—"Go, boil Lord Soulis and ye list, but let me hear no more of him." No sooner said than done—

"On a circle of stones they placed the pot,
On a circle of stones but barely nine;
They heated it red and fiery hot,
Till the burnish'd brass did glimmer and shine.

They roll'd him up in a sheet of lead,
A sheet of lead for a funeral pall;
They plunged him in the cauldron red,
And melted him, lead, and bones and all.

At the Skelfhill, the cauldron still
The men of Liddesdale can show;
And on the spot where they boil'd the pot
The spreat and the deer-hair ne'er shall grow."

At a place called the "Nine Stane Rig" there may still be seen a circle of stones where it is supposed this gruesome tragedy was enacted. The "cauldron red," in which Lord Soulis was boiled, is now in the possession of the Duke of Buccleuch. The Nine Stane Rig derived its name from an old Druidical circle of upright stones, nine of which remained to a late period. Two of these are particularly pointed out as those that supported the iron bar upon which the fatal cauldron was suspended.

The castle of Hermitage ultimately passed into the possession of the Douglasses, and became the principal stronghold of the "Black Knight of Liddisdale," a natural son of the good Lord James Douglas, the trusted friend and companion of Bruce. In the year 1342 it was the scene of the following terrible tragedy:

Sir Alexander Ramsay of Dalhousie, a brave and patriotic Scottish baron, who had specially distinguished himself in the wars with England, was appointed governor of the castle of Roxburgh and Sheriff of Teviotdale. Douglas, who had formerly held the office of Sheriff, was enraged when he heard what had occurred, and vowed revenge against Ramsay, his old companion in arms. He came suddenly upon him with a strong party of his vassals while he was holding his court in the church of Hawick. Ramsay, suspecting no harm, invited Douglas to take a seat beside him. The ferocious warrior, drawing his sword, rushed upon his victim, wounded him, threw him across his horse, and carried him off to the remote and inaccessible castle of Hermitage. There he was thrown into a dungeon, and left to perish of hunger. It is said that his miserable existence was prolonged for seventeen days by some particles of corn which fell from a granary above his prison. Tytler, in commenting on this abominable crime, justly remarks:—"It is a melancholy reflection that a fate so horrid befell one of the bravest and most popular leaders of the Scottish nation, and that the deed not only passed unrevenged, but that its perpetrator received a speedy pardon, and was rewarded by the office which led to the murder."

In later times Hermitage is chiefly associated with the names of Bothwell and Buccleuch. It is still in the possession of the latter noble family, and is one of the most interesting of all the old Border castles.

In the olden time Liddesdale was chiefly inhabited by two numerous and powerful families—the Armstrongs and the Elliots. The laird of Mangerton was the head of the former, and the laird of Redheugh of the latter. Both families were, almost without exception, notorious freebooters. Reiving was the business of their lives. They were inspired, if not with a noble, at least with an overmastering enthusiasm for their nefarious calling. They were strongly of opinion that all property was common by the law of nature, and that the greatest thief was the man who had the presumption to call anything his own! Might was right.

"They may take who have the power,
And they may keep who can."

It was, no doubt, a simple rule, but the consequences resulting from its application were not always of an agreeable description.

It is said that the original name of the Armstrongs was *Fairbairn*, and that the change of name was brought about by a curious incident. The King on one occasion asked a Fairbairn to help him to mount his horse. Stretching out his arm, he caught the King by the thigh, and lifted him into his saddle. From henceforth he was known by the name of *Armstrong*.

The name "Elliot" has undergone considerable changes. It is spelled in some of the older documents in at least seventy or eighty different ways, the most common being Ellwood, Elwald, Elwand, Hellwodd, Halliot, Allat, Elliot. It is remarkable that in many districts in the south of Scotland the name is still pronounced "Allat," though this is one of the older forms in which it appears.

The Elliots and Armstrongs and other inhabitants of Liddesdale attained an unenviable notoriety. The picture which Maitland has drawn of these "Liddesdale Limmers" may be here and there too highly coloured; yet those who are most familiar with the facts of Border history will be the first to admit that it is, on the whole, a fairly accurate description. It is entitled, "A Complaynt against the Thieves of Liddesdale"—

"Of Liddesdale the common thieves,
Sae pertly steals now and reives,
That nane may keep
Horse, nolt, nor sheep
For their mischieves.

They plainly through the country rides,
I trow the mickle devil them guides,
Where they onset
Ay in their gait,
There is no yett,
Nor door them bides.

They leave richt nocht wherever they gae;
There can nae thing be hid them frae;
For gif men wald
Their houses hald,
Then wax they bald
To burn and slay.

They thieves hae near hand herrit hail,
Ettrick Forest and Lauderdale;
Now are they gane
To Lothiane,
And spares nane
That they will wail.

Bot common taking of blackmail,
They that had flesh, and bread, and ale,
Now are sae wrackit,
Made bare and naikit,
Fain to be slaikit,
With water caill.

They thieves that steals and turses hame,
Ilk ane o' them has ane to-name,
Will i' the Laws,
Hab o' the Shaws,
To mak bare wa's
They think nae shame.

They spulyie puir men o' their packs,
They leave them nocht on bed or balks,
Baith hen and cock,
With reel and rock,
The Laird's jock,
All with him taks.

They leave not spindle, spoon, nor speit,
Bed, blanket, bolster, sark, nor sheet,
John o' the Park
Rypes kist and ark;
For all sic wark
He is richt meet.

He is weel kenned, Jock o' the Syde—
A greater thief did never ride;
He never tires
For to break byres;
O'er muir and mires,
Ower guid ane guid.

Of stouth though now they come guid speed,
That nother of God or man has dread;
Yet or I dee,
Some shall them see
Hing on a tree,
While they be dead."

It is evident from this graphic account that these "Liddesdale limmers" were not particular as to their booty. They carried off everything that came to hand, on the principle, perhaps, that if they had no particular use for some of the things they appropriated, they were at least leaving their enemies poorer than when they found them. We read of one John Foster of Heathpool, servant to Sir John Foster, complaining of John Elliot of the Heughehouse, Clement Croser, "Martin's Clemye," John Croser, "Eddie's John," Gib Foster of Fowlesheiles, &c., to the number of thirty, "who stole six oxen, 6 kye, 4 young nowte, ane horse, a nag, a sword, a steil cap, a dagger and knives, 2 spears, 2 dublets, 2 pair of breeches, a cloke, a jerkyne, a woman's kertle and a pair of sleaves, 9 kerchers, 7 railes, 7 partlettes, 5 pair of line(n) sheitis, 2 coverlettes; 2 lynne sheits; a purs and 6/- in monie; a woman's purs and 2 silke rybbons; a windinge clothe; a feather bed; a cawdron, a panne, 4 bond of hempe, a pair of wool cards, 4 children's coates, &c., &c."

The list of goods here "appropriated" by John Elliot and his friends is an interesting one, as it shows "that all was fish that came to their net"—not even the "winding cloth" being discarded when ransacking the house. We also find an account of one Robert Rutherford of Todlaw producing a "remission for art and part of the theft of certain cuschies of silk, sheits, fustiane, linen cloths, scarfs, fustiane, scarfs, and other clothes, furth of the Kirk of Jedworthe—Robert Turnbull of Blindhalche becoming surety to satisfy parties." Sacrilege was of frequent occurrence. We also find the following entry in Pitcairn:—"Remission to Edward Tayt, for the thiftwise breking of the Kirk of Hendirland, and takin away of certaine guids, gold and silver, fra Sir Wilzeame Jurdane." This happened in the year 1493, which points to the fact that at that date the church of Henderland, which stood on the rounded eminence near Henderland farm house, where "Perys and Marjorie Cockburn" have found their last resting place, was then in existence. This place of worship must have disappeared about the time of the Reformation.

These items of information, curious though they may appear, must not be regarded as abnormal instances of the rapacity of the Liddesdale thieves, or "limmers"—to use the designation of an old Act of the Scottish Parliament. They simply denote ordinary incidents of Border reiving. "Kist" and "ark" were made to yield up their treasures. "Insight gear" included everything to be found within the four walls of the house. The very children were sometimes carried off! When the thieves had completed their task those whom they had plundered were occasionally left in a state of absolute destitution. They might congratulate themselves when they were able to keep their clothes on their backs! Some, indeed, were not so fortunate; and, after an encounter with the thieves, were compelled to face the rigour of a severe climate with an exceedingly primitive outfit.

It is interesting to find that the clan system prevailed on the Borders, especially in the south-west portion of the district. In Liddesdale, in the district known as the Debateable land, and along the shores of the Solway, the inhabitants were grouped into clans, many of them numerous and powerful. According to Skene, "the word clan signifies children or descendants, and the clan name thus implies that the members of it are, or were supposed to be, descended from a common ancestor or eponymus, and they were distinguished from each other by their patronymics, the use of surnames in the proper sense of the term being unknown among them. These patronymics, in the case of the *Caenncine*, or chief, and the *Ceanntighs*, or heads of the smaller septs, indicated their descent from the founder of the race or sept; those of the members of it who were of the kin of the Chief or Chieftain showed the personal relation; while the commonality of the clan simply used a derivative form of the name of the clan, implying merely that they belonged to it.".

This form of government, so essentially patriarchal in its nature, is at once the most simple and universal. It is derived from the most primitive idea of authority exercised by a father over his family. Among nations of a Celtic origin this system was universal. Indeed, it is generally held that it is a system peculiar to Celtic tribes. How it came to be established on the Borders is a question which is not easily solved. Sir Walter Scott is of opinion that the system was originally derived from the inhabitants of the western portion of Valentia, who remained unsubdued by the Saxons, and by those of Reged, and the modern Cumberland. He says that the system was not so universal on the eastern part of the Marches, or on the opposite Borders of England. There were many families of distinction who exercised the same feudal and territorial authority that was possessed by other landlords throughout England. But in the dales of Rede and Tyne, as well as in the neighbouring county of Cumberland, the ancient custom of clanship prevailed, and consequently the inhabitants of those districts acted less under the direction of their landlords than under that of the principal men of their name.

It is important that this fact should be kept steadily in mind, as the mode of government, of living, and of making war, adopted by the Borderers on both sides, seems to have been in great measure the consequence of the prevailing system of clanship.

It is the simplest of all possible systems of government. The Chief was not only the legislator and captain and father of the tribe, but it was to him that each individual of the name looked up for advice, subsistance, protection, and revenge.

In "Skene's Acts of Parliament" a Roll of the Border clans is given, from which it would appear that there were seventeen distinct septs, or families, mostly in the south-western portion of the Scottish Borders. The *Middle March* was inhabited by Elliots, Armstrongs, Nicksons, and Crosiers. The *West March* by Scotts, Beatisons, Littles, Thomsones, Glendinnings, Irvinges, Belles, Carrutherses, Grahams, Johnstones, Jardines, Moffettes, and Latimers. These clans are described as having "Captaines, Chieftaines, quhome on they depend, oft-times against the willes of their Landislordes." "Ilk ane o' them," according to Maitland, had a to-name, or *nickname*, as it is commonly called now-a-days. This was a matter of necessity, as otherwise it would have been exceedingly difficult to distinguish the different members of the sept. These to-names are often suggestive and amusing, as most of them are based on some physical or moral peculiarity. In the year 1583 Thomas Musgrave sent an interesting letter to Burghley, Chancellor to Queen Elizabeth, in which he gives a list of the Armstrongs and Elliots. "I understand," he says, "that your lordship is not well acquainted with the names of the waters, and the dwelling places of the riders and ill-doers both of England and Scotland.... May it please, therefore, your lordship to understand, that the ryver Lyddal is a fayre ryver, and hath her course doun by Lyddisdall, so as the dale hath the name of the ryver.... I shall therefore set downe the Ellottes of the head of Lyddall as my skyll will afforde, that your lordship may know the better when their deeds shall come in question. The Ellotes of Lyddisdall:—Robin Ellot of the Redheugh, Chiefe of the Ellottes; Will Ellot of Harskarth his brother; Gebbe Ellot his brother; Adam Ellot of the Shaws; Arche Ellot called Fyre the brayes; Gybbe Ellot of the Shawes; Gorth Simson; Martin Ellot called Rytchis Martin. All these are Robin Ellotes brethren, or his men that are daly at his commandement. The grayne of the Ellotes called the Barneheedes:—Joke Ellot called Halfe loges. The grayne of the Ellottes of the Bark:—Sims Johne Ellot of the Park; Will Ellot, gray Willie; Hobbe Ellot called Scotes Hobbe; Johne Ellot of the Park; Jem Ellot called gray Wills Jeme; Hobbe Ellot called Hobbs Hobbe. The grayne of Martin Ellot of Bradley:—Gowan Ellot called the Clarke; Hobbe Ellot his brother; Arche Ellot his brother; Joke Ellot called Copshawe; John Ellot of Thornesope; Will Ellot of the Steele; Dand Ellot of the Brandley; John Ellot of the same; Seme Ellot of Hardin. All theise Ellots and manie more of them are at Robin Ellot's commandment and dwell betwixt the Armstrongs in Lyddisdall and Whethough town—fewe of them married with Englishe women." Then follows a long list of the "Armstrongs of Mangerton," and of the "Howse of Whetaughe Towre." Some of the names in the list are amusingly suggestive—"Seme Armestronge lord of Mangerton married John Foster's daughter of Kyrshopefoot; Joke Armestronge called the "lord's Joke" dwelleth under Dennyshill besides Kyrsope in Denisborne, and married Anton Armestrong's daughter of Wylyare in Gilsland; Johne

Armestronge called "the lordes Johne," marryet Rytche Grayme's sister.... Thomas Armestrong called "the lordes Tome."... Runyon Armestrong called "the lordes Runyon."... Thom Armestronge Sims Thom, married Wat Storyes daughter of Eske, called Wat of the Hare ends."

We also read of "Thomas Abye," "Gawins Will," "Red Andrew," "Bangtale," "Ould Hector of Harlaw," "Stowlugs," "Cokespoole," "Skinabake," "Carhand," "Hob the Tailor," "Redneb," &c.

Among the Elliots we find such to-names as "Long John," "John the Child," "John Cull the spade," "Bessie's Wife's Riche," "Robin the Bastard of Glenvoren," &c. One of the family of Nixon was known as "Ill Drooned Geordie," a name which seems to indicate that the person who bore it had had at one time or another a narrow escape from what perhaps was his righteous doom. "Wynking Will," "Wry-Crag," "David the Leddy," and "Hob the King," are sufficiently explicit.

These are a fair sample of the *to-names* by which the thieves of Liddesdale were distinguished. It must be admitted, however, that many of them are not quite so respectable as those given, and would hardly admit of reproduction in a modern book. The men to whom they were assigned must have been regarded, one would naturally suppose, as utterly disreputable characters, even by those who associated with them in the invidious calling to which they were devoted.

It is probable that the men of Liddesdale were to a certain extent corrupted by their propinquity to the lawless hordes which inhabited the Debateable land. This was a tract of country lying between the Esk and the Sark, of some fifty or sixty square miles in extent, which was regarded as belonging neither to the one kingdom nor the other. Here the "Genius of Misrule," for many generations, held all but undisputed sway. The Græmes, Littles, and Bells, and other "broken men" of equally unenviable reputation, found in this district a convenient centre for conducting their marauding exploits. It was a matter of no moment to them whether their victims belonged to the one country or the other. They were as destitute of patriotism as of the other virtues. When they were hard driven by the English, they claimed the protection of the Scottish warden; and when he in his turn had accounts to settle with them, they appealed to his English rival in office to shield them from vengeance. In this way they often succeeded in escaping the punishment due to their misdeeds, where others, less happily circumstanced, would have been speedily compelled to "underlie the law." In course of time this state of matters became intolerable, and it was resolved by the Scottish Council in the year 1552 that this district should be divided, the one part to be placed under the jurisdiction of England, the other under that of Scotland. Accordingly, a Commission, on which were representatives of both nations, was appointed to settle, if possible, this long-standing difficulty. These commissioners were allowed the utmost freedom of judgment in fixing upon a proper boundary line, as both governments were agreed that minor difficulties, as to the extent of territory to be allocated to the one country or the other, should not be allowed to stand in the way. The final decision was not so easily arrived at as might, in the circumstances, have been expected. The Scots drew the line considerably to the south, the English to the north, of the boundary finally agreed upon. After considerable discussion, a line was ultimately fixed which satisfied both parties, and a turf dyke was built, stretching from the Sark to the Esk, which is still known as the Scots Dyke.

This was an important step. The boundary was finally settled. The wardens knew the precise limits to which their power and authority extended, and were thus in a position to discharge the duties of their office with more assured certainty of success. But, as might have been anticipated, the fixing of a boundary line did not eradicate, or even to any great extent restrain, the thieving propensities of the lawless inhabitants of this district. The Debateable land continued to nourish "ane great company of thieves and traitores, to the great hurt and skaith of the honest lieges" as in times by-past. But a good beginning had been made in fixing the boundaries, and in course of time more favourable results ensued.

It would be unwarrantable to assert that the Liddesdale thieves attained their unenviable notoriety entirely owing to their intimate association with the fierce banditti to whom reference has been made. The Armstrongs and Elliotts needed no encouragement in the carrying on of their nefarious business of plunder. They were evidently heartily in love with their calling, and were never happier than when engaged in a marauding expedition. But apart from the fact that "evil communications corrupt good manners," the near neighbourhood of the Debateable land constituted an indirect incentive to crime. In the great deer forests of the Highlands there are what are called "sanctuaries," or places to which the deer may resort to escape the huntsman. We are told that when they are disturbed on the mountains, they at once make for the protected area, where they know they are safe from pursuit. The Debateable land constituted for generations just such a "sanctuary," or place of refuge for Border thieves. Here they were comparatively safe. The district formed a little kingdom by itself. Within this region the law was comparatively powerless.

But we find that the "Liddesdale limmers" were occasionally driven to bay in the most effectual manner. Sir Robert Cary on one occasion gave them a salutary lesson, which they did not soon forget. The Armstrongs especially, a powerful and turbulent clan, had long carried things with a high hand on the English Border, burning, despoiling, and slaying to their hearts' content. This state of matters had at last become intolerable, and Cary determined to have it out with them. He called the gentlemen of the neighbourhood together, and acquainted them with the miseries which had been brought upon the people by the rapacity and cruelty of the Liddesdale thieves. They advised him to apply to the Queen and Council for assistance, but this he was unwilling to do, as he thought he was quite able, with the resources at his command, to effectually suppress the lawless horde which had wrought such havoc within his wardenry. He says:—"I told them my intention what I meant to do, which was, 'that myself, with my two deputies, and the forty horse that I was allowed, would, with what speed we could, make ourselves ready to go up to the wastes, and there we would entrench ourselves, and lie as near as we could to the outlaws; and, if there were any brave spirits among them, that would go with us, they should be very welcome, and fare and lie as well as myself: and I did not doubt before the summer ended to do something that should abate the pride of these outlaws.'" With this comparatively small force he set out for Liddesdale. He built a fort on a hill in the immediate vicinity of Tarras moss, into which the thieves, when they learned of his approach, had fled for refuge. Here Cary and his men stayed from the middle of June till near the end of August. The country people supplied him with provisions, being well paid for anything they brought to him. "The chief outlaws," he says, "at our coming, fled their houses where they dwelt, and betook themselves to a large and great forest, (with all their goods,) which was called the Tarras. It was of that strength, and so surrounded with bog and marsh grounds, and thick bushes and shrubs, as they feared not the force nor power of England or Scotland, so long as they were there. They sent me word, that I was like the first puff of a haggis, hottest at the first, and bade me stay there as long as the weather would give me leave. They would stay in the Tarras-wood, till I was weary of lying in the waste; and when I had had my time, and they no whit the worse, they would play their parts, which should keep me waking next winter. Those gentlemen of the country that came not with me, were of the same mind; for they knew, (or thought at least,) that my force was not sufficient to withstand the fury of the outlaws. The time I stayed at the fort I was not idle, but cast, by all means I could, how to take them in the great strength they were in. I found a means to send a hundred and fifty horsemen into Scotland, (conveighed by a muffled man, not known to any of the company,) thirty miles within

Scotland; and the business was so carried, that none in the country took any alarm at this passage. They were quietly brought to the backside of the Tarras, to Scotland-ward. There they divided themselves into three parts, and took up three passages which the outlaws made themselves secure of, if from England side they should at any time be put at. They had their scouts on the tops of hills, on the English side, to give them warning if at any time any power of men should come to surprise them. The three ambushes were safely laid, without being discovered, and, about four o'clock in the morning, there were three hundred horse, and a thousand foot, that came directly to the place where the scouts lay. They gave the alarm; our men broke down as fast as they could into the wood. The outlaws thought themselves safe, assuring themselves at any time to escape; but they were so strongly set upon on the English side, as they were forced to leave their goods, and to betake themselves to their passages towards Scotland. There was presently five taken of the principal of them. The rest, seeing themselves, as they thought, betrayed, retired into the thick woods and bogs, that our men durst not follow them, for fear of losing themselves. The principal of the five, that were taken, were two of the eldest sons of Sim of Whittram. These five they brought me to the fort, and a number of goods, both of sheep and kine, which satisfied most part of the country, that they had stolen them from....

Thus God blessed me in bringing this great trouble to so quiet an end; we broke up our fort, and every man retired to his own house." Judging from this account, one is led to suppose that the force which Cary had at his command was comparatively small. He tells us that he took a list of those that offered to go with him, and found that with his officers, gentlemen, and servants there would be about two hundred good men and horse; a competent number he thought for such a service. But we find in a letter which he sent to Cecil that he speaks of having "a 1000 horse and foot." But whatever may have been the strength of the forces at his command, it is quite certain that, on this occasion at least, he proved himself more than a match for the "Lewd Liddesdales."

The tradition of this famous raid, which was long preserved in the district, differs considerably from the account here given. "The people of Liddesdale have retained," says the editor of the "Border Minstrelsy," "the remembrance of *Cary's raid*," as they call it. "They tell that, while he was besieging the outlaws in the Tarras, they contrived, by ways known only to themselves, to send a party into England, who plundered the warden's lands. On their return, they sent Cary one of his own cows, telling him that, fearing he might fall short of provisions during his visit to Scotland, they had taken the precaution of sending him some English beef."

The anecdote is worth preserving, as it indicates how anxious the Liddesdale reivers were to forget one of the most unpleasant episodes in their history, or at least to make their discomfiture appear in as favourable a light as possible.

X.

AFTER THE HUNTING.

"Efter the hunting the King hanged Johnie Armstrong."
Pitscottie.

"Here is ane cord baith grit and lang,
Quhilk hangit Johne Armstrang,

66

Of gude hempt soft and sound,
Gude haly pepil, I stand ford,
Whaevir beis hangit wi' this cord,
Neidis never to be drowned!"

Sir David Lindsay.

We have already seen that the Armstrongs were a numerous and powerful clan, and that for a considerable period they had been known on the Borders as "notour thieves and limmers." They levied blackmail over a wide district, and appropriated whatever came readiest to hand with a sublime indifference either to neighbourhood or nationality.

"They stole the beeves that made them broth
From Scotland and from England both."

King James V. having succeeded in shaking himself free from the tyranny of the Douglasses, resolved that he would "daunton" the Border thieves, by making them feel the weight of his sword. He made an excellent beginning. He imprisoned the Earls of Bothwell and Home, Lord Maxwell Scott, Ker of Ferniherst, Scott of Buccleuch, Polworth, Johnston, and Mark Ker. It must have been quite evident to the young King, and his counsellors, that so long as these Chiefs were at liberty it would be a bootless errand to proceed against those who owned them allegiance. The ringleaders must first of all be disposed of, and so they were put in ward, there to await his Majesty's pleasure. This measure was not devised, as some suppose, for the purpose of crushing the nobility. It is absurd to infer that James, a youth of seventeen, had projected a deep political plan of this nature. The outrages which these men had committed during his minority had excited his lively resentment, and he was determined that they should no longer maintain bands of lawless followers at the public expense. This necessary measure for the pacification of the Borders was wisely devised, and promptly executed, and must have produced a deep impression, if not a wholesome fear, in the minds of those whom it was intended to influence.

It was in the month of June, 1529, that James set out for Meggatdale, accompanied by eight thousand men, lords, barons, freeholders, and gentlemen, all well armed, and carrying with them a month's provisions. The King commanded all gentlemen that had "doggis that were guid" to bring them with them to hunt "in the said bounds." The Earls of Huntley, Argyle, and Athol, brought their deerhounds with them, and hunted with his Majesty. They came to Meggat, near St. Mary's Loch, and, during their short stay in this district, eighteen score of deer were slain.

The tradition is that on this occasion the King captured William Cockburn of Henderland, a famous freebooter, and hanged him over his own gate. It is quite certain, however, that in regard to this matter the tradition is unreliable. In "Pitcairn's Criminal Trials" we find it stated, under date May 26th—nearly a month before the King left Edinburgh—that "William Cockburne of Henderland was convicted (in presence of the King) of High Treason committed by him, in bringing Alexander Forrestare and his son, Englishmen, to the plundering of Archibald Somervile: And for treasonably bringing certain Englishmen to the lands of Glenquhome: And for Common Theft, Common Reset of Theft, outputting and inputting thereof.—Sentence. For which causes and crimes he has forfeited his life, lands, and goods, moveable and immoveable, which shall be escheated to the King.—Beheaded." Such is the brief but authentic record. It establishes beyond controversy the fact that Cockburn was apprehended, and tried, before the King had left Edinburgh on his famous expedition. The tradition that he was hanged over his own gate, must therefore be set aside.

The Cockburns were an old and well-known family. One of the Scotts of Buccleuch married a daughter of the house, which, on the principle of heredity, may help to explain the well-known reiving propensities of some branches of this famous clan. In "Pitcairn's Criminal Trials," where so much of the ancient history of the great Border families may be read, if not with pleasure, at least not without profit, mention is made of various Cockburns who distinguished themselves as daring and successful freebooters. In the old churchyard of Henderland there is still to be seen a large slab bearing the inscription— "Here lyis Perys of Cockburne and Hys wife Marjory." There is no date on the tombstone, but the likelihood is that this "Perys of Cockburne" was a descendant of the William Cockburn whose fate we have just mentioned.

But the most interesting tradition in connection with this family relates to the well-known ballad, "The Border Widow's Lament," one of the most beautiful, and certainly the most pathetic, of all the Border ballads. It has been supposed to describe the feelings of Cockburn's widow when her husband was put to death by the King.

"My love he built me a bonnie bower,
And clad it a' wi' lilye flour,
A brawer bower ye ne'er did see,
Than my true love he built for me.

There came a man, by middle day,
He spied his sport, and went away;
And brought the King that very night,
Who brake my bower, and slew my knight.

He slew my knight, to me sae dear;
He slew my knight, and poin'd his gear;
My servants all for life did flee,
And left me in extremitie.

I sew'd his sheet, making my mane;
I watch'd the corpse, myself alane;
I watch'd his body, night and day;
No living creature came that way.

I took his body on my back,
And whiles I gaed, and whiles I sat;
I digg'd a grave, and laid him in,
And happ'd him with the sod sae green.

But think na ye my heart was sair,
When I laid the moul' on his yellow hair;
O think na ye my heart was wae,
When I turned about, awa' to gae?

Nae living man I'll love again,
Since that my lovely knight is slain;

Wi' yae lock o' his yellow hair,
I'll chain my heart for evermair."

This exquisite ballad has probably no connection with Cockburn of Henderland,—we feel strongly convinced it has not,—but it is none the less interesting, as it is a composition which can well afford to be regarded apart altogether from its traditional associations.

There is another tradition which it may be as well to notice in passing. It is said that, after hanging Cockburn, the King proceeded to Tushielaw to deal in like manner with Adam Scott, well known on the Borders as "The King of Thieves." His castle stood on the spur of a hill opposite the Rankleburn, on the west side of the river Ettrick, commanding a wide out-look in almost every direction. Near it was the famous "Hanging Tree," which was accidentally destroyed by fire only a few years ago, where the unlucky captives of this noted outlaw were unceremoniously suspended in order to prevent their giving further annoyance. It is said that, on one of the branches, a deep groove was worn by the swaying to and fro of the fatal rope. It would have been most fitting had this cruel marauder been put to death where so many of his victims ended their career. But in this instance the tradition, that this actually happened, has been proved to be without any foundation in fact. We find in "Pitcairn" an account of Adam Scott's trial and execution in Edinburgh. On the 18th May, 1529—just two days after Cockburn had "justified the law"—"Adam Scott of Tuschilaw was Convicted of art and part of theftuously taking *Black-maill*, from the time of his entry within the Castle of Edinburgh, in Ward, from John Brown, Hoprow: And of art and part of theftuously taking *Black-maill* from Andrew Thorbrand and William, his brother: And of art and part of theftuously taking of *Black-maill* from the poor Tenants of Hopcailzow: And of art and part of theftuously taking *Blackmaill*, from the poor Tenants of Eschescheill." Then follows the significant word—"Beheaded."

The King, therefore, when he passed the castle of Tushielaw with his retinue, on his way to Teviotdale to meet Johnie Armstrong, must have had the satisfaction of knowing that Adam Scott had gone "where the wicked cease from troubling."

He had sent a loving letter, written with "his ain hand sae tenderly," to the laird of Gilnockie, requesting him to meet his "liege lord" at a place called Carlenrig on the Teviot, some nine miles above Hawick. Various accounts have been given by historians, both ancient and modern, as to the means adopted by the King to bring about Armstrong's capture and execution. Leslie, for example, informs us that "all this summer the King took great care to pacify the Borders with a great army, and caused forty-eight of the most noble thieves, with Johnie Armstrong, their captain, to be taken and hanged on growing trees." He says that "George Armstrong, brother of the said Johnie, was pardoned and reserved alive, *to tell on the rest*, which he did, and in course of time they were apprehended by the King, and punished according to their deserts." Pinkerton, who evidently bases his account largely on the information supplied by Leslie, enters more fully into particulars. He alleges that "by the assistance of George, his brother, who was pardoned on condition of betraying the others, John Armstrong, the chief of the name, whose robberies had elevated him to opulence and power, was captured and suffered the fate of a felon." These statements, definite though they are, ought not to be lightly accepted, as the strongest reasons may be advanced against this supposition. In the first place, we ought to remember that, however many sins and shortcomings the Border reivers may be accused of, breach of faith can hardly be reckoned one of them. "Hector's Cloak" was a phrase of peculiar opprobrium. It was regarded as the symbol of meanness and perfidy. That this one instance of betrayal should have been so long remembered, and so thoroughly detested, is an unmistakable indication that the Border thieves, bad as they were in many respects, were not without a high sense of honour in matters of this kind. It is hardly conceivable, therefore, that Armstrong's brother could have been guilty of his betrayal. Strong proof would require to be forthcoming in support of such a statement; and this is precisely what the historians do not give us.

But there are other and more cogent arguments against this view. George Armstrong was under no necessity of betraying his brother in order to save himself. He could easily have escaped had he been minded to do so. The King's authority did not extend beyond the Scottish Border. It is morally certain, had Armstrong and his friends ever suspected that James would have treated them as he did, they would either have taken refuge in their own strongholds and defied him, or crossed the Border into England, where they would have been comparatively safe from pursuit. That they did neither, but voluntarily came before the King, is strong evidence in favour of the supposition that they were enticed by fair promises to place themselves within his power. The very fact that Armstrong neither sought nor obtained a safe conduct goes to prove that he had the most implicit confidence in the clemency, if not the goodwill, of his sovereign. There was no betrayal on the part of anyone, save the King himself. This is clearly brought to view in the peculiarly graphic and fascinating account which "Pitscottie" has given of this memorable incident. He says:—"Efter this hunting the King hanged Johnie Armstrong, laird of Gilnockie, quhilk monie Scottis man heavilie lamented, for he was ane doubtit man, and als guid ane chiftane as ever was upon the borderis, aither of Scotland or of England. And albeit he was ane lous leivand man, and sustained the number of xxiiij. weill horsed able gentlemen with him, yitt he nevir molested no Scottis man. Bot it is said, from the Scottis border to Newcastle of England, thair was not ane of quhatsoevir estate bot payed to this John Armstrong ane tribut to be frie of his cumber, he was sae doubtit in England. So when he entred in befoir the King, he cam verie reverentlie, with his foresaid number verie richlie apparrelled, trusting, that in respect he had cum to the Kingis grace willinglie and voluntarilie, not being tain nor apprehendit be the King, he sould obtaine the mair favour. Bot when the King saw him and his men so gorgeous in their apparrell, and so many braw men under ane tirrantis commandement, throwardlie, he turned about his face, and bad tak that tirrant out of his sight, saying, 'Quhat wantis yon knave that a King should have.' But when Johnie Armstronge perceaved that the King kindled in ane furie againes him, and had no hope of his lyff, notwithstanding of many great and fair offeris, quhilk he offerred to the King, that is, that he sould sustene himself with fourtie gentlemen, ever readie to awaitt upon his majestie's service, and never tak a pennie of Scotland, nor Scottis man. Secondlie, that there was not ane subject in England, duik, earle, lorde, or barrun, bot within ane certane day he sould bring ony of them to his majesty, either quick or dead. He seing no hope of the Kingis favour towards him, said verrie proudlie, 'I am bot ane fooll to seik grace at ane graceles face. But had I knawin, sir, that ye wad have taken my lyff this day, I sould have leved upon the borderis in disphyte of King Harie and yow baith; for I knaw King Harie wold doun weigh my best hors with gold to knaw that I were condemned to die this day.' So he was led to the scaffold, and he and his men hanged. This being done, the King returned to Edinburgh, the xxiiij. day of July, and remained meikle of that winter in Edinburgh."

This interesting and picturesque account is corroborated by another historian, who says: "On the eighth of June the principalls of all the surnames of the clannes on the Borders came to the King upon hope of a proclamation proclaimed in the King's name that they sould all get their lyves, if they would come in and submit themselves to the King's will, and so upon this hope Johnie Armstrang, who keipit the castle of Langhame (a brother of the laird of Mangerton's, a great thieff and oppressor, and one that keiped still with him four-and-twenty well-horsed men), came to the King, and another called Ill Will Armstrong, another stark thieff, with sundrie of the Scotts and Elliotts, came all forward to the campe where the King was in hopes to get their pardons. But no sooner did the King persave them, an that they were cum afarre off, when direction was given presentlie to enclose them round about, the which was done accordinglie, and were all apprehendit, to the number of threttie fyve persons, and at a place called Carlaverocke. Cheapell, were all committed to the gallowes. One Sandy Scot, a prowd thieff, was brunt because it was provin that he haid brunt a pure widowes house, together with sum of her children. The English people were exceeding glade when they understood that John Armstrang was executed, for he did great robberies and stealing in England, menteaning 24 men in houshold evorie day upon rieff and oppression. The rest delyvered pledges for their good demeanare in tymes to cum." There can be little doubt that Armstrong was cruelly betrayed, not by his brother, but by the King—a circumstance which seriously reflects on his honour and good name.

The suggestion has been made that this expedition against the laird of Gilnockie was undertaken by James at the instigation of Lord Maxwell, who was then a ward in Edinburgh. It is certainly a somewhat suspicious circumstance that three days after Armstrong's execution Maxwell received from the King the gift of all the property, moveable and immoveable, which pertained to "umquhill Johne Armstrang, bruther to Thomas Armstrang of Mayngerton, and now perteining to our souverane lord be reason of eschete throw justefying of the said umquhill Johnie to the deid for thift committed be him." As might be expected, when all the circumstances were taken into consideration, the execution of Armstrong and his followers produced a profound sensation, and a deep and bitter feeling of resentment. It was long believed by the peasantry of the district that, to mark the injustice of the deed, the trees on which they were hanged, withered away. On purely abstract grounds it may be argued that Armstrong and his men richly deserved the punishment meted out to them, but this fact does not exonerate the King from the charge of treachery and deceit which has justly been brought against him. The measures he adopted to capture the quarry were unworthy of a puissant monarch with eight thousand well armed men under his command. He might well have paid more respect to the principles of honour and fair play.

It is interesting to find that the version of Armstrong's capture and execution given in the famous ballad agrees substantially with the accounts of Pitscottie and Anderson. There, we are told, that the King sent a "loving letter" to Armstrong, inviting him to a conference.

The King he wrytes a luving letter,
With his ain hand sae tenderly,
And he hath sent it to Johnie Armstrang,
To cum and speik with him speedily.

This communication evidently excited no suspicion, and extensive preparations were at once made to extend to his Majesty a kind and hearty welcome. It was even hoped that he might be induced to dine at Gilnockie!

The Eliots and Armstrangs did convene;
They were a gallant cumpanie—
"We'll ride and meet our lawful King,
And bring him safe to Gilnockie.

"Make kinnen and capon ready, then,
And venison in great plentie;
We'll welcum here our royal King;
I hope he'll dine at Gilnockie!"

71

They ran their horse on the Langholme howm,
And brak their spears wi' mickle main;
The ladies lukit frae their lofty windows—
"God bring our men weel hame again!"

When Johnie cam before the King,
Wi' a' his men sae brave to see,
The King he movit his bonnet to him;
He ween'd he was a King as well as he.

According to the balladist, it would seem that Armstrong's ruin was brought about by the princely style in which he appeared before his sovereign. The King, highly displeased, turned away his head, and exclaimed—

"Away, away, thou traitor strang!
Out o' my sight soon mayst thou be!
I grantit never a traitor's life,
And now I'll not begin wi' thee."

This unexpected outburst of indignation led Armstrong at once to realise the perilous position in which he found himself placed. He now felt that, if his life was to be spared, he must use every means in his power to move the King to clemency. Consequently he promised to give him "four-and-twenty milk white steeds," with as much good English gold "as four of their braid backs dow bear;" "four-and-twenty ganging mills," and "four-and-twenty sisters' sons" to fight for him; but all these tempting offers were refused with disdain. As a last resource, he said—

"Grant me my life, my liege, my King!
And a brave gift I'll gie to thee—
All between here and Newcastle town
Sall pay their yeirly rent to thee."

This was no idle boast. So powerful had Armstrong become that, it is said, he levied black-mail—(which is only another form of the word "*black-meal*," so-called from the conditions under which it was exacted)—over the greater part of Northumberland. But even the prospect of increasing his revenue by accepting this tribute was not sufficient to turn the King aside from his purpose. He was bent on Armstrong's destruction, a fact which now became painfully evident to the eloquent and generous suppliant. Enraged at the baseness of the King, he turned upon him and gave vent to the pent up feelings of his heart—

"Ye lied, ye lied, now King," he says,
"Altho' a King and Prince ye be!
For I've luved naething in my life,
I weel dare say it, but honesty—

"Save a fat horse, and fair woman,
Twa bonny dogs to kill a deir,
But England suld have found me meal and mault,
Gif I had lived this hundred yeir!

"She suld have found me meal and mault,
And beef and mutton in a' plentie;
But never a Scots wyfe could have said,
That e'er I skaith'd her a puir flee.

72

"To seik het water beneith cauld ice,
Surely it is a greit folie—
I have asked grace at a graceless face,
But there is nane for my men and me!
"But had I kenn'd ere I cam frae hame,
How thou unkind wadst been to me!
I wad have keepit the Border side,
In spite of all thy force and thee.

"Wist England's King that I was ta'en,
O gin a blythe man he wad be!
For anes I slew his sister's son,
And on his briest bane brak a trie."

The balladist then proceeds to give a minute description of the dress worn by the redoubtable freebooter on this occasion—of his girdle, embroidered and bespangled with gold, and his hat, with its nine targets or tassels, each worth three hundred pounds. All that he needed to make him a king was "the sword of honour and the crown." But nothing can now avail.

"Farewell! my bonny Gilnock hall,
Where on Esk side thou standest stout!
Gif I had lived but seven yeirs mair,
I wad hae gilt thee round about."

John murdered was at Carlinrigg,
And all his gallant companie;
But Scotland's heart was ne'er sae wae,
To see sae mony brave men die.

It was a foul deed, foully done. The King was no doubt determined, as it is said, to "make the rush bush keep the cow," and perhaps to a certain extent he succeeded, as some time after this, Andrew Bell kept ten thousand sheep in Ettrick Forest, and they were as safe as if they had been pasturing in Fife or the Lothians. But the murder of Armstrong in no way daunted the other members of that notable clan. Many of them took refuge on the English side of the Border, and for years waged a successful predatory warfare against their *quondam* Scottish neighbours. In 1535, for example, we find that "Christopher Armstrong, Archibald his son, Ingram Armstrong, Railtoun, Robert and Archibald Armstrong there, John Elwald, called *Lewis John*, William, son of Alexander Elwald, and Robert Carutheris, servants to the laird of Mangerton; John Forrestare, called *Schaikbuklar*, Ninian Gray his servant, Thomas Armstrong in Greneschelis, *Lang Penman*, servant of one called *Dikkis Will*. Thomas Armstrong of Mangerton, and Symeon Armstrong, called *Sim the Larde*" and several others, were denounced rebels, and their whole goods escheated for not underlying the law for having stolen from John Cockburn of Ormiston seventy "drawand oxen" and thirty cows; and for art and part of traitorously taking and carrying off three men-servants of the said John, being the keepers of the said castle, and "detaining them against their will for a certain space;" and further "for art and part of the Stouthreif from them of their clothes, whingars, purses and certain money therein." Indeed the depredations of the clan after the execution of Gilnockie were on the most extensive scale. On the 21st February, 1536, Symon Armstrong was "convicted of art and part of the theft and concealment of two oxen from the laird of Ormistone, furth of the lands of Craik, and a black mare from Robert Scott of Howpaslot, furth of the lands of Wolcleuche; committed during the time he was in the King's ward, about Lammas 1535. *Item*, of art and part of the theft and concealment of five score of cows and oxen from the said laird of Ormistone, stolen furth of the said lands of Craik; committed by *Evil-willit Sandie*, and his accomplices, in company with Thomas Armstrong, *alias Greneschelis*, and Robert Carutheris, servants of the said Symon, and certain Englishmen, at his command, common Thieves and Traitors, on July 27, 1535. *Item*, of art and part of the traitorous *Fire-raising* and *Burning of the Town of Howpaslot*; And of art and part of the Theft and Concealment the same time of sixty cows and oxen belonging to Robert Scott of Howpaslot and his servants; committed by Alexander Armstrong, in company with Robert Henderson, *alias Cheyswame*,. Thomas Armstrong, *alias* Grenescheles, his servants, and their accomplices, common Thieves and Traitors, of his causing and assistance, during the time he was within the King's ward, upon October 28, 1535. *Item*, of art and part of the theft and concealment of certain sheep from John Hope and John Hall, the King's shepherds, furth of the lands of Braidlee in the Forest; committed during the time he was within the said ward. *Item*, for art and part of the treasonable assistance given to Alexander Armestrang, called *Evil-willit Sandy*, a sworn Englishman, and sundry other Englishmen his accomplices, of the names of Armestrangis, Niksounis, and Crosaris, in their treasonable acts. Sentence—To be drawn to the gallows and Hanged thereupon: And that he shall forfeit his life, lands, possessions, and all his goods, moveable and immoveable, to the King, to be disposed of at his pleasure." In the following month John Armstrong, *alias Jony of Gutterholes*, and Christopher Henderson were hanged for "Common Herschip and Stouthreif, Murder and Fire-raising." These items give but a faint idea of the extent to which the Armstrongs carried on their depredations.

But, perhaps, a still more serious result of the unwise policy adopted by James in his treatment of the Armstrongs, was the destruction of that feeling of loyalty to the Scottish Crown, which had hitherto been, in some measure at least, a characteristic of the Borderers. Henceforth not only the Armstrongs, but many others besides, were ready to place their arms and their lives at the service of the English government, and to take part with their ancient foes in oppressing and despoiling their own countrymen. In the battle of Ancrum Moor in 1546, there was a considerable contingent of Scottish Borderers fighting under the standard of Lord Eure, and it was only after the tide of war had turned in favour of the Scots that they threw away the badge of foreign servitude and helped to complete the victory. It maybe said that in acting thus they were moved simply by considerations of personal advantage. Be this as it may, the incident clearly shows that their attachment to King and country had been all but completely destroyed. Had James acted with ordinary discretion and foresight he might at once have secured the end he had in view, and at the same time have won over to his side, and to the side of law and order, a body of men whose crimes were due rather to the peculiarity of their circumstances than to their own inherently evil dispositions. He had a great opportunity, but he failed conspicuously to take advantage of it. He learned, when it was too late, that force, when not wisely applied, may produce greater evils than those it seeks to remedy.

XI.

THE CORBIE'S NEST.

"Where are ye gaun, ye mason lads,
Wi' a' your ladders, lang and hie?"
"We gang to berry a corbie's nest

That wons not far frae Woodhouselee."
Kinmont Willie.

The incidents in the predatory warfare so long carried on by the dwellers on both sides of the Border were not all of a painful or tragic character. The spirit of fun sometimes predominated over the more selfish and aggressive instincts. There was a grim kind of humour characteristic of the Border reiver. He certainly was not disposed to laugh on the slightest provocation,—his calling was much too serious for that,—but when he once relaxed, his mirth was not easily controlled. And, however degrading his occupation may have been in its general tendency, there was often displayed among the Border thieves, even among the very worst of them, a spirit of the most splendid heroism, which helps to redeem the system from the general contempt in which it is regarded by the moralist of modern times. Many of the leaders were not only men of undaunted courage, but of considerable military genius. In a later age, under other and happier conditions, they would have won renown on many a well-fought battlefield. They possessed the qualities, physical and moral, of which great soldiers are made. The Bold Buccleuch, Little Jock Elliot, Johnie Armstrong of Gilnockie, and his kinsman, Willie of Kinmont— not to mention other names which readily occur to the mind in this connection—were men dowered by nature with great courage and resource. They were strong of arm and dauntless of heart. We do not seek to justify their deeds. These were reprehensible enough, judged by almost any standard you may apply to them. But just as some people find it impossible to smother a certain sneaking kind of admiration of the Devil, so magnificently delineated in Milton's "Paradise Lost"—a being who seems possessed of almost every quality save that of consecrating his varied endowment to worthy ends—so in like manner it is difficult to withhold a certain meed of admiration for some of the "nobil thieves" whose names stand out prominently in, if they cannot always be said to adorn, this long chapter of Border history. They were undoubtedly men of ability, energy, and force of character, who would have won their spurs in almost any contest into which they had chosen to enter.

One of the most notable of this band was the famous Kinmont Willie, renowned in Border song and story. He was an Armstrong, a descendant of the laird of Gilnockie, whom James VI. put to death at Carlinrig in such graceless fashion. He, like all his race, was a notorious freebooter. The English Border, more especially the West and Middle Marches, suffered much at his hands. He had a large and well armed following, and conducted his marauding expeditions with an intrepidity and skill which created a feeling of dismay among the subjects of his oppression. Nor did it matter much to him where, or on whom, he raided. The King's treachery at Carlinrig had destroyed—at least so far as the Armstrongs and their friends were concerned—the last lingering spark of patriotism. Their hand was now turned against every man, English and Scottish alike. They had become pariahs, outcasts, whose only ambition was revenge. But bad as Kinmont was, and his record is of the worst, it might be said of him, as it was said of one of the greatest and best men Scotland has ever produced, that "he never feared the face of man." He was always to the front, dealing out hard blows; courting danger, but never dreaming of defeat. He cared as little for the warden as for the meanest and most defenceless subject of the realm. Scrope tells us, for example, that on one occasion "certain goods were stolen by Scottish men from one of the Johnstones, a kinsman of the laird Johnstone being warden, whereupon the fray arose, and the warden himself, with his company and friends, pursued the same. But Kinmont and his complices being in the way to resist them, the warden and his company returned again to Annand, the which he taketh in very yll parts.".

It was no doubt a sore point with the warden that he should be thus interfered with in this masterful fashion, and one can readily sympathise with him in his chagrin. Such an incident shows that Kinmont and his friends were in a position to set the constituted authorities at defiance, and conduct their reiving "without let or hindrance." The warden, however, was not altogether free from blame for this state of matters. He seems to have given the thieves every encouragement as long as they confined their depredations to the English Border. Scrope, in a letter to Walsingham, informs him that "as well in the tyme of my being with you, as also synce my return home, manye and almost nightlie attemptates have been committed in Bewcastle and elsewhere within this wardenrie, as well by the Liddesdales as also by the West Wardenrie of Scotland, specially Kinmont, his sonnes and complices; who ... are nevertheless at their pleasure conversaunte and in company with the warden, and no part reprehended for their doynges." Hunsdon, another English warden, even goes the length of suggesting that the King himself (James VI.) privately encouraged Kinmont in his evil doing. He says that four hundred horse came to "Hawden brigges," and took up the town and burned divers houses, whereat the King was very angry, "because it was done there—for he would have had it to be done in some part of my wardenry. Since the taking up of Hawden brigg, Will of Kinmont, who was the principal man who was at it, hath been with the King in his cabinet above an hour, and at his departure the King gave him 100 crowns, as littell as he hath. What justis wee are to looke for att the King's hands lett her Majestie judge!".

Thus encouraged by the warden and the King, it is not to be wondered at that Kinmont should have thrown himself with great enthusiasm into the work of harassing and plundering all who came within his power.

But his name might have remained in comparative obscurity, notwithstanding his depredations, had it not been for an extraordinary incident which occurred, and for which he was in no way directly responsible.

The dramatist has said that some men are born great, and that others have greatness thrust upon them. We are not prepared to say that only the latter part of the statement applies to the subject of our sketch, for, despite his evil-doing, Kinmont was a man of much natural ability—ability amounting almost to genius. But that he had "greatness thrust upon him" will be readily conceded. His name will always remain associated with one of the most thrilling incidents in Border history. The circumstance which made him famous was this. He had been present at Dayholm, near Kershopefoot, on the occasion of a day of truce, in the month of March, in the year 1596. The business which called them together having been finished, he was returning home, accompanied by a few of his friends, along the banks of the Liddle, when he was suddenly attacked by a body of two hundred English Borderers, led by Salkeld, the deputy of Lord Scrope, the warden of the East March, chased for some miles, captured, tied to the body of his horse and thus carried in triumph to Carlisle castle.

They band his legs beneath the steed,
They tied his hands behind his back;
They guarded him, fivesome on each side,
And they brought him ower the Liddel-rack.

They led him thro' the Liddel-rack,
And also through the Carlisle sands;

They brought him to Carlisle castell,
To be at my Lord Scrope's commands.

This proceeding was clearly in direct violation of Border law, which guaranteed freedom from molestation to all who might be present at a warden court, or day of truce, betwixt sunrise on the one day and sunrise on the next. We can easily understand the overmastering desire of the warden's deputy to lay Kinmont "by the heels," as he had long been notorious for his depredations on the English Border, but it is incumbent on the representatives of the law that they should honour it in their own persons, and, however many crimes might be laid to the charge of the famous freebooter, he was justly entitled to enjoy the freedom, which a wise legal provision had secured, even to the greatest offenders. The excuse given by Scrope for this manifest breach of Border law is an exceedingly lame one. He says:—"How Kinmont was taken will appear by the attestations of his takers, which, if true, 'it is held that Kinmont did thereby break the assurance that daye taken, and for his offences ought to be delivered to the officer against whom he offended, to be punished according to discretion.' Another reason for detaining him is his notorious enmity to this office, and the many outrages lately done by his followers. He appertains not to Buccleuch, but dwells out of his office, and was also taken beyond the limits of his charge, so Buccleuch makes the matter a mere pretext to defer justice, 'and do further indignities.'".

That Kinmont had broken the assurance taken at the warden court is an assertion in support of which neither has "takers," nor Scrope give a scintilla of proof. Had such a thing really happened, there surely would have been no difficulty in establishing the fact; but this is not done, or even attempted to be done, by those whose interest it was to prove the accusation up to the hilt. The other reasons adduced for this unwarrantable proceeding will not bear serious consideration. That Kinmont bore no goodwill to Scrope or those associated with him in his office, may be taken for granted; and that he and his friends and associates had been guilty of many outrages on the English Border, goes without saying. But a slight examination of the excuses will be sufficient to show that they are mere subterfuges. The point in dispute is carefully left out of view by the English warden. No doubt Kinmont richly deserved to suffer the utmost penalty of the law on the ground of his misdemeanours; but he had been present at the warden court, where he would never have gone had he not felt sure that he was amply protected from arrest by the law to which we have referred. It may be said that nearly every man present on that occasion, irrespective of nationality, might have been apprehended on the same general grounds. To use an expressive Scottish phrase—"they were all tarred with the same stick." It was therefore a direct violation, not only of the spirit, but of the letter of Border law, for Salkeld to take Kinmont prisoner. Scrope was clearly in the wrong—a fact of which he himself seems dimly conscious—as he displayed an amount of temper and irritability in dealing with the case which seemed to indicate that he felt the weakness of his position. On the other hand, the "rank reiver," who had been thus suddenly and unceremoniously "clapped in jail," accepted the situation with a singular amount of philosophical indifference. He felt sure that the deed would not go unavenged, that his friends, and he had many of them, would leave no stone unturned in order to effect his release. The balladist finely represents him as saying—

My hands are tied, but my tongue is free,
And whae will dare this deed avow?
Or answer by the Border law?
Or answer to the bold Buccleuch?

"Now haud thy tongue, thou rank reiver!
There's never a Scot shall set thee free;

Before ye cross my castle yate,
I vow ye shall take farewell o' me."

"Fear na ye that, my lord," quo' Willie;
"By the faith o' my body, Lord Scroope," he said,
"I never yet lodged in hostelrie,
But I paid my lawing before I gaed."

An account of what had happened was speedily conveyed to Branxholme, where the
Bold Buccleuch was residing. When he heard what had occurred he was highly indignant.
The picture drawn by the balladist is graphic in the extreme. For intense realism it has
rarely ever been surpassed—

He has ta'en the table wi' his hand,
He garr'd the red wine spring on hie—
"Now Christ's curse on my head," he said,
But avenged on Lord Scroope I'll be!

"O is my basnet a widow's curch?
Or my lance a wand o' the willow-tree?
Or my arm a ladye's lilye hand,
That an English lord should lightly me!

"And have they ta'en him, Kinmont Willie,
Against the truce of Border tide?
And forgotten that the bauld Buccleuch
Is Keeper here on the Scottish side?

"And have they e'en ta'en him, Kinmont Willie,
Withouten either dread or fear?
And forgotten that the bold Buccleuch
Can back a steed, or shake a spear?

"O were there war between the lands,
As well I wot that there is none,
I would slight Carlisle castell high,
Though it were builded of marble stone.

"I would set that castell in a low,
And sloken it with English blood!
There's never a man in Cumberland,
Should ken where Carlisle castell stood.

"But since nae war's between the lands,
And there is peace, and peace should be;
I'll neither harm English lad or lass,
And yet the Kinmont freed shall be!"

Before resorting to extreme measures Buccleuch did everything in his power to bring
about an amicable settlement of the case. He first of all applied to Salkeld for redress; but
Salkeld could only refer him to Lord Scrope, who declared that Kinmont was such a
notorious malefactor that he could not release him without the express command of
Queen Elizabeth. Buccleuch then brought the matter under the consideration of James,

who made an application through an ambassador, for Kinmont's release; but this also proved unavailing.

It looked as if the imprisoned freebooter was likely to pay his "lodging mail" in a very unpleasant fashion. The English government seemed determined to detain him until such times as they could conveniently put a period to his career by hanging him on Haribee hill. But Buccleuch, while anxious to effect his purpose, if possible by constitutional means, was determined that Kinmont should be rescued, whatever might be the method he was under the necessity of adopting. To accomplish his purpose he was prepared to "set the castle in a low, and sloken it with English blood." This threat was regarded as a mere piece of bravado. The castle was strongly garrisoned and well fortified. It was in the centre of a populous and hostile city, and under the command of Scrope, who was regarded as one of the bravest soldiers in England. The Bold Buccleuch, however, was not easily daunted. He had a strong arm and a brave heart, and he knew that he could summon to his aid a small band of followers as brave and resolute as himself. On a dark tempestuous night, two hundred of his bravest followers met him at the tower of Morton, a fortalice in the Debatable land, on the water of Sark, some ten miles or so from Carlisle. Their plans had been carefully considered and determined upon a day or two before, when they had met at a horse race near Langholm. The Armstrongs, of course, were ready to adventure their lives in such a laudable undertaking, and the Græmes, to whom Will of Kinmont was related by marriage, were also forward with promises of assistance. They were all well mounted—

With spur on heel, and splent on spauld,
And gleuves of green, and feathers blue—

and carried with them scaling ladders and crowbars, hand-picks and axes, prepared to take the castle by storm. The rain had been falling heavily, and the Esk and the Eden were in roaring flood, but boldly plunging through their turbid waters they soon came within sight of the "Corbie's Nest" which they had come to "herry," and—

The first o' men that we met wi',
Whae sould it be but fause Sakelde?

"Where be ye gaun, ye hunters keen?"
Quo' fause Sakelde; "Come tell to me?"
"We go to hunt an English stag,
Has trespass'd on the Scots countrie."

"Where be ye gaun, ye marshall men?"
Quo' fause Sakelde; "Come tell me true!"
"We go to catch a rank reiver,
Has broken faith wi' the bauld Buccleuch."

But the troublesome questions of the "fause Sakelde" were speedily cut short by the lance of Dickie of Dryhope, who led the band—

Then nevir a word had Dickie to say,
Sae he thrust the lance through his fause bodie.

The way was now clear for the advance upon the castle. Everything seemed favourable to the success of their hazardous undertaking. The heavens were black as pitch, the thunder rolled loud and long, and the rain descended in torrents—

"But 'twas wind and weet, and fire and sleet,
When we came beneath the castle wa'."

When Buccleuch and his men reached the castle they were dismayed to find that the ladders they had brought with them were too short; but finding a postern they undermined it, and soon made a breach big enough for a soldier to pass through. "In this way a dozen stout fellows passed into the outer court (Buccleuch himself being fifth man who entered,) disarmed and bound the watch, wrenched open the postern from the inside, and thus admitting their companions, were masters of the place. Twenty-four troopers now rushed to the castle jail, Buccleuch meantime keeping the postern, forced the door of the chamber where Kinmont was confined, carried him off in his irons, and sounding their trumpet, the signal agreed on, were answered by loud shouts and the trumpet of Buccleuch, whose troopers filled the base court. All was now terror and confusion, both in town and castle. The alarum-bell rang and was answered by his brazen brethren of the cathedral and the town house; the beacon blazed upon the top of the great tower; and its red, uncertain glare on the black sky and the shadowy forms and glancing armour of the Borderers, rather increased the terror and their numbers. None could see their enemy to tell their real strength.".

The suddenness of the attack and the terrific noise made by Buccleuch and his troopers as they laid siege to the castle, created confusion and dismay amongst the defenders of the stronghold. Lord Scrope, with commendable prudence, kept close within his chamber. He was convinced, as he afterwards declared, that there were at least five hundred Scots in possession of the castle.

Kinmont, as he was borne triumphantly forth on the broad shoulders of Red Rowan, shouted a lusty "good night," to his bewildered lordship.

Then Red Rowan has hente him up
The starkest man in Teviotdale—
"Abide, abide now, Red Rowan,
Till of my Lord Scroope I take farewell."

"Farewell, farewell, my gude Lord Scroope!
My gude Lord Scroope, farewell he cried—
I'll pay you for my lodging maill,
When first we meet on the Border side."

Then shoulder high, with shout and cry,
We bore him down the ladder lang;
At every stride Red Rowan made,
I wot the Kinmont airns play'd clang!

"O mony a time" quo' Kinmont Willie,
"I've prick'd a horse out oure the furs;
But since the day I back'd a steed,
I never wore sic cumbrous spurs!"

Having now successfully accomplished their purpose, Buccleuch and his men moved off towards the place where they had left their horses, and in a short time they were safely back on Scottish soil—

Buccleuch has turn'd to Eden Water,
Even where it flow'd frae bank to brim,
And he has plunged in wi' a' his band,
And safely swam them through the stream.

He turn'd them on the other side,
And at Lord Scroope his glove flung he—

"If ye like na my visit in merry England,
In fair Scotland come visit me."

A cottage on the roadside between Longtown and Langholm, which stands close to the Scotch Dyke, is still pointed out as the residence of the smith who was employed, on this occasion, to knock off Kinmont Willie's irons. It is said that when Buccleuch arrived he found the door locked, the family in bed, and the knight of the hammer so sound a sleeper, that he was only wakened by the Lord Warden thrusting his long spear through the window, and nearly spitting both Vulcan and his lady.

The rescue of Kinmont Willie—a most notable feat from whatever point of view it may be regarded—made Buccleuch one of the most popular heroes of the age. It was declared on all hands that nothing like it had been accomplished since the days of Sir William Wallace.

According to a statement made in the "Border Papers," Buccleuch was assisted in effecting Kinmont's rescue by Walter Scott of Goldielands; Walter Scott of Harden; Will Elliot of Gorronbye; John Elliot of Copeshawe; the laird of Mangerton; the young laird of Whithaugh and his son; three of the Calfhills, Jock, Bighames, and one Ally, a bastard; Sandy Armstrong, son to Hebbye; Kinmont's Jock, Francie, Geordie, and Sandy, all brethern, the sons of Kinmont; Willie Bell, "Redcloak," and two of his brethren; Walter Bell of Goddesby; three brethren of Tweda, Armstrongs; young John of the Hollows, and one of his brethren; Christie of Barngleish and Roby of Langholm; the Chingles; Willie Kange and his brethren with their "complices."

The breaking of the castle, and the rescue of Kinmont, completely upset the equanimity of my Lord Scrope. His indignation almost unmanned him. He wrote a long letter to the Privy Council describing the circumstances, and denouncing Buccleuch and his accomplices, in no measured terms. He entreated the Council to induce her Majesty to call upon the King of Scotland to deliver up Buccleuch "that he might receive such punishment as her Majesty might find that the quality of his offence merited." He assured their lordships that "if her Majesty shall give me leave it shall cost me both life and living, rather than such an indignity to her Highness, and contempt to myself, shall be tolerated." From the subsequent correspondence on this subject, which was of a voluminous nature, one can easily see that Scrope was more concerned about the indignity to himself than the contempt which had been offered to her Majesty. He seems to have found it more difficult than he at first anticipated to move the government to take prompt and effective action. Buccleuch, as may be readily supposed, had a good deal to say in his own defence. He argued, and with considerable cogency, that Kinmont's capture and imprisonment constituted a gross violation of Border law, and that he had not made any attempt at his rescue until he had exhausted every other means of accomplishing his purpose. He also pointed out that the representations which he had made had been received with scant courtesy, and that even the remonstrance of the King had been treated with contempt. Further, he showed that his Borderers had committed no outrage either on life or property, although they might have made Scrope and his garrison prisoners, and sacked the city.

These considerations ought to have weighed heavily in Buccleuch's favour, but Elizabeth would listen to no excuses. She demanded his immediate surrender. For a time James refused to comply, and was warmly supported by the whole body of his council and barons, even the ministers of the Kirk were strongly opposed to surrender. Had the King been able to act with as much freedom as some of his predecessors, it is morally certain that this demand would have been indignantly repelled, but in the circumstances he had to proceed with caution, as he was afraid that resistance might lead to unpleasant results. And so, bowing to the inevitable, Buccleuch was surrendered—at least he was for a time put in ward in Blackness.

The letter which Elizabeth addressed to James on this occasion is written throughout in the most passionate language. It is evident that Her Majesty had great difficulty in controlling her feelings. After soundly rating her "Dear brother" on the attitude he had assumed, she says:—"Wherefore, for fine, let this suffice you, that I am as evil treated by my named *friend* as I could be by my known *foe*. Shall any castle or habytacle of mine be assailed by a night larcin, and shall not my confederate send the offender to his due punishment? Shall a friend stick at that demand that he ought rather to prevent? The law of kingly love would have said, nay: and not for persuasion of such as never can or will stead you, but dishonour you to keep their own rule, lay behind you such due regard of me, and in it of yourself, who, as long as you use this trade, will be thought not of yourself ought, but of conventions what they will. For, commissioners I will never grant, for an act that he cannot deny that made; for what so the cause be made, no cause should have done that. And when you with a better weighed judgment shall consider, I am assured my answer shall be more honourable and just; which I expect with more speed, as well for you as for myself.

For other doubtful and litigious causes in our Border, I will be ready to point commissioners, if I shall find you needful; but for this matter of so villainous a usage, assure you I will never be so answered, as hearers shall need. In this and many other matters, I require your trust to our ambassador, which faithfully will return them to me. Praying God for your safe keeping. Your faithful and loving sister, E. R."

Such plain speaking might not be relished by the Scottish King, but the interests at stake were too great to enable him to disregard it. He was in thorough sympathy with Buccleuch, but he dare not resist further, and so pacified the angry Queen by yielding her demands.

XII.

FLAGELLUM DEI.

"Then out and spak the nobil King,
And round him cast a wilie ee—
Now, had they tongue, Sir Walter Scott,
Nor speak of reif nor felonie:
For, had every honest man his awin kye,
A right puir clan thy name wad be!"

Ballad of the Outlaw Murray.

hile reflecting great credit on the prowess of the Bold Buccleuch, the rescue of Kinmont Willie gave rise to many serious local as well as international complications. As we have seen, the English Queen was deeply offended. She resented the high-handed and arbitrary manner in which the release of this famous prisoner had been effected. It constituted a gross insult to the Crown, and she was determined that those responsible for the deed should suffer for their temerity. The anger of Elizabeth was no trifling matter under any circumstances, but to James, whose courage was never a conspicuous quality, it was dreaded in the last degree. He simply quailed before the storm, and hastened to tender his humble submission. The Queen received his assurances of contrition with commendable graciousness. Yet it would seem she was not quite satisfied. Buccleuch had been put in ward, but he had not been, as was demanded, surrendered to the English government, and satisfaction was apparently out of the question until this condition had been complied with. She expostulated with James on the impropriety of the course he had seen fit to adopt, and gave him an interesting lecture on the manner in which he ought to discharge the duties of his high office. "For the punishment given to the offender," she says, "I render you many thanks; though I must confess, that without he be rendered to ourself, or to our warden, we have not that we ought. And, therefore, I beseech you, consider the greatness of my dishonour, and measure his just delivery accordingly. Deal in this case like a king, that will have all this realm and others adjoining see how justly and kindly you both will and can use a prince of my quality; and let not any dare persuade more for him than you shall think fit, whom it becomes to be echoes to your actions, no judgers of what beseems you.

For Border matters, they are so shameful and inhuman as it would loathe a king's heart to think of them. I have borne for your quiet too long, even murders committed by the hands of your own wardens, which, if they be true, as I fear they be, I hope they shall well pay for such demerits, and you will never endure such barbarous acts to be unrevenged.

I will not molest you with other particularities; but will assure myself that you will not easily be persuaded to overslip such enormities, and will give both favourable ear to our ambassador, and speedy redress, with due correction for such demeanour. Never think them mete to rule, that guides without rule.

Of me make this account, that in your world shall never be found a more sincere affection, nor purer from guile, nor fuller fraught with truer sincerity than mine; which will not harbour in my breast a wicked conceit of you, without such great cause were given, as you yourself could hardly deny; of which we may speed, I hope, *ad calendas Græcas*.

I render millions of thanks for such advertisements as this bearer brought from you; and see by that, you both weigh me and yourself in a right balance; for who seeks to supplant one, looks next for the other."

These wise and weighty admonitions were no doubt received in a becoming spirit. But James was not prepared at once to comply with the demand that Buccleuch should be handed over to the tender mercies of his enemies. Buccleuch was a special favourite. He was disposed, therefore, to shield him as long as he could conveniently do so, with any degree of safety to himself and his own interests. Negotiations were carried on between the two governments for a period of eighteen months, and everything might have been amicably settled had the wardens, and others in authority, only conducted themselves with a reasonable amount of discretion. Scrope, especially was dying to be revenged on those who had subjected him to such great indignity; and consequently, a few months after the castle of Carlisle had been broken into by Buccleuch, he gathered together two thousand men and marched into Liddesdale, where he and his followers created great devastation. They burned, so the Scottish commissioners allege, "24 onsettes of houses, and carried off all the goods within four miles of bounds. They coupled the men their prisoners 'tua and tua togeather in leashe like doggis. Of barnis and wemen, three or four scoore, they stripped off their clothis and sarkis, leaving them naked in that sort, exposit to the injurie of wind and weather, whereby nyne or tenne infantes perished within eight daies thereafter.'"

The answer of the English commissioners to this indictment indicates, at least, the grounds on which Scrope regarded himself as justified in undertaking this invasion of Liddesdale. The reasons adduced are plausible, if not always convincing. "It is no novelty," they say, "but an ancient custom, for the English warden to assist his opposite, and the keeper of Liddesdale, to ride on and 'herrie' such thieves, and on occasion to do so at his own hand.... Buccleuch, besides (1) surprising the second fortress of the Queen's Border; (2) slaying 24 of her subjects, including 16 of her soldiers; (3) has bound himself with all the notorious riders in Liddesdale, Eskdale, and Ewesdale, and after asserting that he paid 'out of his own purse' half of the sworn bill of Tyndale of £800, which the King commanded him to answer, joined himself with the Ellotts and Armstrongs, to plunder Tyndale for demanding the balance, slaying in their own houses 7 of the Charletons and Dodds the chief claimants. And being imprisoned by the King, he made a sporting time of it, hunting and hawking, and on his release did worse than ever, maintaining his 'coosens' Will of Hardskarth, Watt of Harden, &c., to murder, burn, and spoile as before.

The people under his charge, Ellotts, Armstrongs, Nicksons, &c., have of late years murdered above 50 of the Queen's good subjects, many in their own houses, on their lawful business at daytime—as 6 honest Allandale men going to Hexham market, cut in pieces. For each of the last 10 years they have spoiled the West and Middle Marches of £5000. In short, they are intolerable, and redress being unattainable, though repeatedly demanded by the Queen and warden, the justifiable reprisal ordered by her Majesty in necessary defence of her own Border, cannot in equity be called an invasion, but rather 'honourable and neighbourlike assistance,' to maintain the inviolable amitie between the princes and realms, against the proud violaters thereof in eyther nation.... To conclude— this action of the Lord Scrope's is to be reputed and judged a 'pune,' an ancient Border tearme, intending no other than a reprisall, which albeit of late years her Majesty's peacable justice hath restrained."

There is much in a name. This invasion of Liddesdale, resulting in the burning of numerous homesteads, the slaughter of many women and children, accompanied by barbarities of the most revolting description, is euphoniously described by the commissioners as "honourable and neighbourlike assistance." The women and bairns, who were led in leashes like so many dogs, were no doubt duly grateful to my Lord Scrope and his minions for their kindly attentions! The absurdity of such a verdict is surely unique.

It would appear that Buccleuch's enforced absence from the Borders, after the taking of Carlisle castle, was of brief duration. He was soon back in his old haunts, and at his old trade. What had happened in the interim was not likely to enhance his feeling of regard for Scrope, and those who were aiding and abetting him in this matter. He was determined to avenge the cruel raid which had been made upon Liddesdale. Along with Sir Robert Ker of Cessford, another renowned freebooter, he marched into Tynedale with fifty horse and a hundred foot, burned at noonday three hundred onsteads and dwelling houses; also barns, stables, ox houses, &c., to the number of twenty; and murdered "with the sworde" fourteen who had been to Scotland, and brought away their booty. The English warden was utterly helpless. He dare not lift a finger to stay the progress of the invaders. He gave vent to his feelings in a letter to Burghley, in which he says—"To defend such like incursions, or rather invasions, with sorrow as formerly I declare to your lordship the weak state of Tindale, for there was not 6 able horse to follow the fray 'upon the shoute,' though in daytime, and where as reported to me, there were 300 able foot, 'or better,' there was not a hundred of this following, 'and those naked.' This piteous state increases since my coming, and I cannot see how to amend it, leaving this to your wisdom, 'wishing to God' I had never lived to serve where neither her Majesty nor her officer is obeyed; fearing unless assisted by her Majesty's forces, Tyndale will be laid waste as other parts of the March are."

One cannot restrain a certain feeling of commiseration for the English warden, who was so shamefully neglected by his government, and so miserably supported in the discharge of his duties by those dwelling within his wardenry. The complaint which Eure here makes is one which was often made by the wardens on the English Border. They were frequently left in a comparatively helpless condition, having neither men, horses, nor money sufficient for their purposes. The knowledge of this fact no doubt encouraged the Scots to pursue their nefarious calling with a boldness and persistency, which, at first sight, appear somewhat extraordinary.

Buccleuch, when charged with the atrocities here so minutely described, had a good deal to say in his own defence. He avowed that his inroad on Tynedale was fully justified. He says—"60 English entered Liddesdale by night, slew 2 men, and drove many sheep and cattle, when the fray arising, he with neighbouring gentlemen 'followed the chace with the dog,' and put the first men he met making resistance, to the sword. The rest of the spoil, taken to sundry houses in Tindale, was therein held against him by the stealers, and though he offered them life and goods, if the cattle were delivered, he had to force entry by the firing of doors, when the houses were burned 'besides his purpose,' with the obstinate people who refused to yield on trust."

This plausible story, the main facts of which, however, are admitted by the English warden, did not go far to pacify the Queen of England. She threatened the utmost penalties unless Buccleuch and Ker were delivered up to her. The time had gone past for further "excuses, deferrings, and lingerings." It is said her resentment had reached such a pitch that, with her concurrence, a plan was formed to *assassinate* Buccleuch.

Though the Queen had at first been opposed to the appointment of a Commission for the consideration of some of the more important questions which had arisen between the two kingdoms, owing mainly to Buccleuch's exploits, she ultimately yielded the point, and it is an interesting and significant fact that during the time of the sitting of the Commission Buccleuch was busily engaged in ravaging with fire and sword some of the fairest districts within the English Border. The magnitude of his offences had evidently impressed them. They hardly knew what to say about him. In the first paragraph of the report which they issued we read:—"We have accomplished the treaty of the Border causes with all the diligence possible, though not to so great advantage to the realm as we desired. Yet we have revived articles of the former treaties discontinued, supplied many old defects, and made new ordinances. Slaughters we were forced to leave as they were (the Scots protesting that they could not, under their instructions, deal with them); but we trust as the punishment is left to the princes, her Majesty will so consider the same, that it shall be found far better that we have left that article at large, than if we had condiscended to any meane degree of correccion for so barbarous acts ... specially by Baklugh, who is *flagellum Dei* to his miserably distressed and oppressed neighbours."

But, however distressing Buccleuch's conduct may have been to the English members of the Commission, it is evident that neither King nor Council in Scotland was disposed to regard him as a "scourge of God." He went up to Edinburgh at this time, when things seemed to be going so much against him in the Commission, and had an interview with James, and so obtained his favourable countenance, that "they laughed a long time on the purpose." The Council took an equally favourable view of the situation, affirming that "it was found that his last invasion of England was just, for 'repetition' of goods stolen a short time before, and the slaughter was but of special malefactors, enemies to the public weal and quiet of both countries."

Elizabeth, however, took a different view of the matter, and put her foot down with such purpose and determination that James speedily became convinced that he must either surrender his favourite, or involve the country in a war with England. The latter alternative was out of the question, as it might have imperilled his claim to the succession, and so Buccleuch was compelled to place himself as a prisoner in the hands of Sir William Bowes, who conducted him to Berwick, and put him in ward, there to await the Queen's pleasure. Sir John Cary was then governor of the town, and it was with much perturbation and many misgivings that he undertook the safe custody of such a notorious and masterful captive. In a pathetic letter which he addressed to Lord Hunsdon, he says—"I entreat your lordship that I may not become the jailor of so dangerous a prisoner, or, at least, that I may know whether I shall keep him like a prisoner or no? for there is not a worse or more dangerous place in England to keep him in than this; it is so near his friends, and besides, so many in this town willing to pleasure him, and his escape may be so easily made; and once out of the town he is past recovery. Wherefore I humbly beseech your honor let him be removed from hence to a more secure place, 'for I protest to the Almighty God, before I will take the charge to keep him here, I will desire to be put in prison myself, and to have a keeper of me!' For what care soever be had of him here, 'he shall want no furtherance whatsoever wit of man can devise, if he himself list to make an escape.' So I pray your lordship, 'even for God's sake and for the love of a brother,' to relieve me from this danger.".

This passionate appeal, to be relieved from the responsibility of taking charge of Buccleuch, does not seem to have received much attention. Buccleuch remained under Cary's guardianship, and, needless to say, proved himself one of the most tractable of prisoners. He could not well have acted otherwise, for he must by this time have become fully convinced that Elizabeth was determined to have her way, and that, in the peculiar circumstances in which the Scottish King was placed, he could ill afford to thwart her wishes. Sir Robert Ker was also induced to place himself in the hands of the English authorities. Strange to relate, he was placed in charge of Sir Robert Cary, with whom he lived for a considerable time on the most intimate and friendly terms. "Contrary to all men's expectations," says Cary, "Sir Robert Car chose me for his guardian, and home I brought him to my own house after he was delivered to me. I lodged him as well as I could, and took order for his diet, and men to attend on him; and sent him word, that (although by his harsh carriage towards me, ever since I had that charge, he could not expect any favours, yet) hearing so much goodness of him, that he never broke his word; if he would give me his hand and credit to be a true prisoner, he would have no guard set upon him, but would have free liberty for his friends in Scotland, to have ingress and regress to him as often as he pleased. He took this very kindly at my hands, accepted of my offer, and sent me thanks.

Some four days passed; all which time his friends came unto him, and he kept his chamber. Then he sent to me, and desired me I should come and speak with him, which I did; and after long discourse, charging and recharging one another with wrongs and injuries, at last, before our parting, we became good friends, with great protestations on his side, never to give me occasion of unkindness again. After our reconciliation, he kept his chamber no longer, but dined and supped with me. I took him abroad with me, at least thrice a-week, a-hunting, and every day we grew better friends. Bocleugh, in a few days after, had his pledges delivered, and was set at liberty. But Sir Robert Car could not get his, so that I was commanded to carry him to York, and there to deliver him prisoner to the archbishop, which accordingly I did. At our parting he professed great love unto me for the kind usage I had shown him, and that I would find the effects of it upon his delivery, which he hoped would be shortly."

Sir Robert Ker was as good as his word. After he had regained his freedom, by the delivery of the pledges demanded, he returned to his duties as warden of the East March, and seems to have conducted himself to the entire satisfaction of his generous opponent. Cary says that they often met afterwards at days of truce, and that he had as good justice as he could have desired—their friendship remaining unbroken to the end.

The fortunes of the "Bold Buccleuch," after his imprisonment in Berwick, were of a varied, but by no means of an unpleasant character. He returned to his duties as Keeper of Liddesdale, and applied himself with energy and ability to the arduous task of keeping his unruly charge, as far as possible, within due bounds of law. This was an almost impossible undertaking, as the Armstrongs and Elliots and other "broken men" of the district had been so long accustomed to a lawless life that they quickly resented any interference with their liberty. The change which had come over the spirit of Buccleuch's dream was not at all to their liking, and consequently they turned against him, and assailed him with much bitterness. He was "in contempt with them" because of his just dealing with Cary. They would gladly have shaken off his yoke, and were privately working for his overthrow, that they might have the "raynes louse" again. But difficult as the task was, Buccleuch was not easily turned aside from his purpose. He had evidently become convinced that a change of policy was desirable in the interests of the country, and he was determined to carry it out, however formidable might be the opposition with which he had to contend. The fact is significant, and ought to be carefully borne in mind. Buccleuch's indiscretions during the earlier part of his official life were manifold, and severely reprehensible. The only defence which can be offered in his behalf is, that he was placed in a position of great responsibility before he was old enough to appreciate to the full extent the consequences of his actions. His extreme youth, fiery temperament, and fervid patriotism, account for many things in his life which otherwise would be difficult either to explain or justify. But if he sinned greatly, he also repented sincerely. It is really to him we owe the first impulse in the social regeneration of the Borders. From 1597 onwards, he contributed more towards the establishment of good order in the district over which he presided—and it was infinitely the worst district in the country— than any other man of his time. It may be said, indeed, that in him many of the finest qualities of the Scottish Borderer came to full fruition. He was brave, resolute, independent, quick to resent injuries, but withal, warm-hearted and generous. We do not greatly wonder at the large place he has filled in the traditional story of the country. His was a powerful and fascinating personality, and though, from a national point of view, the sphere of his activities was comparatively limited, his name is not unworthy of being associated with some of the greatest names in Scottish history.

Towards the close of the year 1599 he went to London to make his peace with the Queen. In a letter to Cecil, written by Sir Robert Cary, we have striking testimony given of the change which had taken place in Buccleuch's attitude towards the English government. "He will be desirous," Cary says, "to kiss the Queen's hand: which favour of late he hath very well deserved, for since my coming into these parts, I do assure your honour he is the only man that hath run a direct course with me for the maintenance of justice, and his performance hath been such as we have great quietness with those under his charge. Nor have I wanted present satisfaction for anything by his people: and he has had the like from me. There is not an unsatisfied bill on either side between us.".

Considering the terms of this letter, we are not surprised to learn that the "Bold Buccleuch" was received at Court with considerable favour. If it be true that Elizabeth at one time was privy to a plot to assassinate him, she must surely have had some qualms of conscience when at last this "stark reiver" stood before her. The scene is a memorable one. The Queen demanded of him, with one of those lion-like glances which used to throw the proudest nobles on their knees, how he dared to storm her castle, to which the Border baron replied—"What, madam, is there that a brave man may not dare?" The rejoinder pleased her; and, turning to her courtiers, she exclaimed—"Give me a thousand such leaders, and I'll shake any throne in Europe!"

XIII

MINIONS OF THE MOON.

"Diana's Foresters, Gentlemen of the shade,
Minions of the Moon."—Falstaff.

"*Reparabit Cornua Phoebe.*"—Motto: Harden Family.

"The siller moon now glimmers pale;
But ere we've crossed fair Liddesdale,
She'll shine as brightlie as the bale
That warns the water hastilie.

"O leeze me on her bonny light!
There's nought sae dear to Harden's sight:
Troth, gin she shone but ilka night,
Our clan might live right royallie."

Feast of Spurs.

he more famous reivers whose names have been handed down in the
traditions, poetry, and history of the Scottish Border, are seldom regarded with any very
pronounced feelings of aversion. The Armstrongs, Elliots, Græmes, Stories, Burneses,
and Bells; the Scotts, Kers, Maxwells, and Johnstones—whose depredations have been
recorded with much fulness of detail in the annals of the country, were no doubt quite as
bad as they have been described. They cannot be acquitted of grave moral delinquencies,
judged even by the standard of the age in which they lived. But at this distance of time
many are disposed to regard their depredations and lawless life, if not with a kindly, at
least with an indulgent eye. It must be frankly admitted that there was an element of
genuine heroism in their lives, which goes far to redeem them from the contempt with
which, under other conditions, we would have been compelled to regard them. What they
did was, as a general rule, done openly, and evidently with a certain sub-conscious
feeling that their actions, if rightly understood, were not altogether blame-worthy. Their
reiving was carried on under conditions which developed some of the best as well as
worst elements of their nature and manhood. The Border reiver, whatever he was, can
certainly not be described as cowardly. He carried his life in his hands. He never knew
when he went on a foraging expedition, whether he might return. The enemy with which
he had to contend was vigilant and powerful. Before he could drive away the cattle, he
had, first of all, to settle accounts with the owner. He might be worsted in the encounter,
and instead of securing his booty, he might find himself a captive, with the certainty of
being strung up on the nearest tree, or drowned in some convenient pool. Such incidents
were of almost every day occurrence. Reiving was therefore one of the most exciting and
hazardous of occupations, demanding on the part of those engaged in it, a strong arm and
a dauntless spirit. The burglar who sneaks up to a house while the inmates are asleep, and
plies his nefarious calling in silence and under shade of night, and is ready to start off,
leaving everything behind him, the moment the alarm is raised, is a contemptible
miscreant, for whom the gallows is almost too mild a form of punishment. But the Border

reiver was made of different metal; was, indeed, a man of an essentially higher type. He was prepared to fight for every hoof or horn he wished to secure. It was a trial of skill, of strength, of resource, with the enemy. No doubt he had occasionally to ride during the night, aided only by the mild rays of the moon. The way was often long, the paths intricate, and the dangers manifold; but he was also prepared, under the full blaze of the noonday sun, to challenge those he had come to despoil, to protect and retain their property if they could. It was open and undisguised warfare on a miniature scale. This, of course, was not true of *all* the reivers on the Borders. Some of them were hardly worthy of their profession. There are black sheep in every trade—men who represent the baser qualities of their kind, and who bring discredit on their associates.

In looking back over the long list of famous reivers there are many names which, somehow or other, we are disposed to regard with a more or less kindly feeling. This may be difficult to explain, but the fact is undeniable. Perhaps the feeling is due, to a certain extent at least, to the fact that, despite the mode of life adopted by these men, they represented many really admirable qualities, both of intellect and heart. Johnie Armstrong of Gilnockie, for example, was one of the most notorious of the clan to which he belonged, and yet he was evidently regarded as a great hero, who had been most shamefully treated by the King. It is also interesting to find that he had a high opinion of himself. He prided himself on his *honesty*. However much injury he had inflicted on the unfortunate Englishmen, who had to bear the brunt of his onslaughts, it gives him infinite pleasure and satisfaction to affirm that "he had never skaithed a Scots wife a puir flee." It is possible, too, that his tragic end may have something to do with the kindly feeling with which his memory is cherished, though this in itself is not sufficient to account for the place he occupies in the Valhalla of Border heroes.

In the same way a halo of romance has gathered round the name of the "Bold Buccleuch," whose spirit of chivalry has gone far to redeem his memory from opprobrium. The penetrating eye of the English Queen was quick to discern in him qualities of a high order which only required the proper sphere for their development. He may well be regarded as a truly great man who was compelled by the circumstances in which he found himself placed, to devote his time and talents to tasks which were quite unworthy of his genius. Hence, when the opportunity occurred, he speedily proved himself not only a great leader of men, but a most potent factor in the social and moral regeneration of the district with which he was so intimately associated.

But of all the Border reivers whose names have been handed down in song and story, none is regarded with more kindly, we might almost say affectionate interest, than that of "Auld Wat of Harden." For many years he played an important part in Border affairs, and was always to the front in harassing and despoiling the English. We have already noticed the assistance he gave his near kinsman, the "Bold Buccleuch," in the assault on Carlisle castle, when Kinmont Willie was so gallantly rescued from imprisonment. But, four years prior to this event, in the year 1592, he took part, under the leadership of Bothwell, in the famous "Raid of Falkland," when the King was surprised in his Palace, and would have had short shrift from the Borderers, had not timely warning been given him of his danger. This escapade entailed on the laird of Harden somewhat serious consequences. An order was issued by the King, with the consent of the Lords of his Council, to demolish the *places, houses, and fortalices* of Harden and Dryhoip, pertaining to the said Walter Scott. The order runs thus—"Apud Peiblis, xiij die mensis Julij, anno lxxxxij (1592)—The Kingis Majestie, with aduise of the Lordis of his Secreit Counsale, Gevis and grantis full pouer and Commission, expres bidding and charge, be thir presentis, to his weil-belouitt William Stewart of Tracquair, to dimoleis and cause to be dimoleist and cassin doun to the ground, *the place and houssis of* Tynneis, quhilkis pertenit to James Stewart sumtyme of Tynneis; as alswa, the lyke pouer and commissioun, expres bidding and charge, to

Walter Scott of Gouldielandis and Mr Iedeon Murray, conjunctlie and seuerallie, to dimoleis and caus be dimoleist and cassin doun to the ground, *the placeis, houssis, and fortalices of* Harden *and* Dryhoip, pertening to Walter Scott of Harden, quha, with the said James Steuart, wes arte and parte of the lait tresonabill fact, perpetrat aganis his hienes awin persone at Falkland: And that the foirsaidis personis caus the premisses be putt in execution with all convenient expeditioun in signne and taikin of the foirsaidis uthiris personis tressounable and unnaturall defection and attemptat, committit be thame in manner foirsaid. As thay will ansuer to his hienes upon thair obedience."

This was a severe blow to the laird of Harden, but he doubtless bore it with that fine philosophical indifference for which he was distinguished. The motto of the Harden family, "We'll hae moonlight again," breathes the spirit of optimism, and indicates that the reverses of fortune were never regarded as irreparable. Hope sprang eternal in the Harden breast!

But Auld Wat was never disposed to linger unduly, even when courting the smile of the capricious Goddess. He believed in himself, and relied mainly for his good fortune on his own energy and skill. He was a man of the world—keen, subtle, far-seeing, energetic—never allowing the grass to grow under his feet. He believed in taking time by the forelock—in making hay while the sun shone. Rarely did he ever miss a favourable opportunity of increasing "his goods and gear." And his reiving was carried on in no paltry or insignificant fashion. He was a man of large ideas, and he carried them out on a splendid scale. For example, we find that in 1596 he ran a day foray into Gilsland, and carried off "300 oxen and kye, a horse and a nag." This was a large addition to make to his stock, and one cannot help thinking that the "dell" in front of Harden castle, where he kept his captured nowte, must have often been unduly crowded. But then it ought be remembered that the demands on his hospitality were numerous and not always easily met. He had a numerous body of retainers, as was befitting a man of his position, who had to be kept in "horse meat and man's meat," and having so many to provide for, his large herds often disappeared with great rapidity. The result was that he was constantly under the necessity of crossing the Border in order to replenish his stock. It is related that on one occasion he overheard the town herd calling out to some one, as he was passing, to "send out Wat o' Harden's coo." "Wat o' Harden's coo!" the old reiver indignantly exclaimed, "My sang, I'll soon mak ye speak of Wat o' Harden's kye," and so he at once gathered his forces, marched into Northumberland, and before long he was seen on his way back driving before him a big herd of cows and a basson'd bull. On his way he passed a large sow-backed haystack. Turning round in his saddle and looking at it wistfully, he said, in a regretful tone of voice, "If ye had four feet, ye wadna stand long there!"

It is perhaps to this successful foray that Lord Eure refers in a letter addressed to Cecil under date July 15, 1596, in which he says:—"Watt Ellatt, *alias* Watt of Harden, with other East Tividale lairds had 300 or 400 able horsemen, laying an ambush of 300 or 400 foote, brake a day forray a myle beneathe Bellinghame, spoiled the townes men in Bellinghame, brake the crosse, toke all the cattell upp the water to the number thre or fower hundred beastes at the leaste, hath slaine three men of name and wounded one allmoste to deathe, fired noe houses. The fray rose and being brought to me at Hexhame about ix° or x° houers in the morning, I rose myself with my household servuantes, caused the beacons to be fired and sent the fray eche way rounde aboute me, and yet could not make the force of the countrie iiij^{xx} horsemen and some six score footmen. I followed with the horsemen within twoe or three myles of Scotland, and except Mr Fenwick of Wellington, together with the Keaper of Tindale, Mr Henry Bowes, ther was not one gentleman of the Marche to accompanie me, or mett me at all; and when all our forces were togeither, we could not make twoe hundredth horsse, nor above twoe hundredth footmen.... With shame and greife I speake it' the Scottes went away unfought withall."

It will thus be seen that within a few months this famous freebooter had transferred from English soil some six or seven hundred head of cattle. No doubt like his neighbours, who were engaged in the same precarious line of business, he had many unsuccessful raids to recount, but he was certainly one of the most wary and successful of the reivers on the Scottish side of the Border.

Sir Walter Scott, who was a descendant of Wat of Harden, has an interesting note in his "Border Minstrelsy" regarding the family. "Of this Border laird," he says, "commonly called *Auld Wat of Harden*, tradition has preserved many anecdotes. He was married to Mary Scott, celebrated in song by the title of 'The Flower of Yarrow.' By their marriage contract, the father-in-law, Philip Scott of Dryhope, was to find Harden in horse meat and man's meat at his Tower of Dryhope for a year and a day; but five barons pledge themselves, that, at the expiry of that period, the son-in-law should remove without attempting to continue in possession by force! A notary-public signed for all the parties to the deed, none of whom could write their names. The original is still in the charter-room of the present Mr Scott of Harden. By 'The Flower of Yarrow' the Laird of Harden had six sons; five of whom survived him, and founded the families of Harden (now extinct), Highchesters (now representing Harden), Reaburn, Wool, and Synton. The sixth son was slain at a fray, in a hunting match, by the Scotts of Gilmanscleuch. His brothers flew to arms; but the old laird secured them in the dungeon of his tower, hurried to Edinburgh, stated the crime, and obtained a gift of the land of the offenders from the Crown. He returned to Harden with equal speed, released his sons, and showed them the charter. 'To horse, lads!' cried the savage warrior, 'and let us take possession! The lands of Gilmanscleuch are well worth a dead son.'"

Hogg's description of "Auld Wat" as he set out for Edinburgh on this occasion is humourously realistic:

And he's awa' to Holyrood,
Amang our nobles a',
With bonnet lyke a girdle braid,
And hayre lyke Craighope snaw.

His coat was of the forest green,
Wi' buttons lyke the moon;
His breeks were o' the guid buckskyne,
Wi' a' the hayre aboon.

His twa hand sword hang round his back,
An' rattled at his heel;
The rowels of his silver spurs
Were of the Rippon steel;

His hose were braced wi' chains o' airn,
An' round wi' tassels hung:
At ilka tramp o' Harden's heel,
The royal arches rung.
......

Ane grant of all our lands sae fayre
The King to him has gien;
An' a' the Scotts o' Gilmanscleuch
Were outlawed ilka ane.

But Harden's best fortune came to him with his wife—the far-famed "Flower of Yarrow."

This beautous flower, this rose of Yarrow,
In nature's garden has no marrow.

So sang Allan Ramsay. And since his day the charms of "Yarrow's Rose" have inspired many a more or less tuneful ode. But Mary Scott's beauty was, after all, not her greatest gift. She was wise beyond most of her sex, and skilful to a degree in the management of her husband. We find, for example, that instead of remonstrating with him on his culpable negligence in allowing the larder to become depleted, she quietly set before him when he came to dinner a pair of clean spurs! The hint thus indirectly conveyed was quite sufficient. Immediately her worthy spouse was in the saddle and riding as fast as his nag could carry him towards the English fells. It is interesting to know that the spurs that were thus suggestively served up for dinner are still in the possession of the family, being carefully preserved among Lord Polwarth's treasures at Mertoun House.

But while Wat of Harden could look after his own interests, he was never unmindful of the interests of others. When the Captain of Bewcastle came over to Ettrick "to drive a prey," and carried off Jamie Telfer's kye, he rendered splendid service in rescuing the herd from the hand of the spoiler. Though Telfer, with "the tear rowing in his ee," pled with the Captain to restore his property, he was only laughed at for his pains—

"The Captain turned him round and leugh,
Said—"Man, there's naething in thy house,
But ae auld sword without a sheath
That hardly now would fell a mouse."

Telfer first of all applied for assistance at Stobs Ha', evidently thinking that he had some special claim on "Gibby Elliot," but he was unceremoniously turned from the door, and told to go to "Branksome" and "seek his succour where he paid blackmail." When Buccleuch heard what had taken place, he cried—

"Gar warn the water, braid and wide,
Gar warn it sune and hastilie!
They that winna ride for Telfer's kye,
Let them never look in the face o' me!"

Auld Wat and his sons having also been informed of the Captain's raid, lost no time in getting out their steeds and hurrying after the English reiver. Over the hills, down near the Ritterford on the Liddel, the melee began. The Captain was determined to drive Jamie Telfer's kye into England despite the opposition of the Scotts, but he was made to pay dearly for his temerity.—

Then til't they gaed, wi' heart and hand,
The blows fell thick as bickering hail;
And mony a horse ran masterless,
And mony a comely cheek was pale.

Willie Scott, the son of Buccleuch, was left dead on the field. When Harden saw him stretched on the ground "he grat for very rage."—

"But he's ta'en aff his gude steel cap,
And thrice he's waved it in the air—
The Dinlay snaw was ne'er mair white
Nor the lyart locks of Harden's hair.

"Revenge! revenge!" Auld Wat 'gan cry;
"Fye, lads, lay on them cruellie!

92

We'll ne'er see Teviotside again,
Or Willie's death revenged sall be."

The conflict was speedily ended. The Captain of Bewcastle was badly wounded, and taken prisoner; his house was ransacked, his cattle driven off, and Jamie Telfer returned to the "Fair Dodhead" with thirty-three cows instead of ten.—

"When they cam' to the fair Dodhead,
They were a wellcum sight to see!
For instead of his ain ten milk kye,
Jamie Telfer has gotten thirty and three.

And he has paid the rescue shot,
Baith wi' goud and white monie:
And at the burial o' Willie Scott,
I wat was mony a weeping ee."

The eldest son of Wat of Harden was destined to become as famous as his father, though in a different way. He had evidently, from what we learn of him, inherited all the reiving tendencies of his race. But the difficulty of crossing the Border had been considerably increased. Buccleuch, the Keeper of Liddesdale, had changed his tactics. He had now begun to use his utmost endeavour to bring about a better understanding, and a better state of feeling, between the two countries. Willie Scott no doubt realised that a raid on the English Border, though successful, might now get the whole family into serious trouble. But the kye "were rowting on the loan and the lea," and something had to be done to augment the quickly vanishing herd. He took into his confidence a farmer, who lived on the banks of the Ettrick—William Hogg—well known as the "Wild Boar of Fauldshope." This redoubtable reiver was a progenitor of the Ettrick Shepherd, whose family, it is said, possessed the lands of Fauldshope, under the Scotts of Harden, for a period of 400 years. He was a man of prodigious strength, courage, and ferocity, and ever ready for the fray. For some reason or other he had a strong antipathy to Sir Gideon Murray of Elibank, the picturesque ruins of whose Castle may still be seen on the banks of the Tweed, a mile or two above Ashiesteel. That young Harden could have no particular liking for him is easily understood, as he was one of the men who had been commissioned by the government to destroy Harden castle as a punishment for the part taken by his father in the Raid of Falkland. Sir Gideon had a splendid herd of cattle pasturing on the green slopes above the Tweed, and so Willie Scott resolved, with the assistance of his powerful coadjutor, to transfer as many of them as possible to his own pastures. The night was set, the expedition was carefully planned, and fortune seemed to smile upon the project. But—

The best laid schemes o' mice and men
Gang aft a glee.

Some one was good enough to convey to Sir Gideon a hint of what was on foot, and he at once took measures to give the thieves, when they came, a warm reception. After a sharp encounter, Willie Scott was taken prisoner, and thrown into the dungeon of the Castle, with his hands and feet securely bound. He knew quite well the fate which awaited him on the morrow. He would be led forth to the gallows, and there made to pay the forfeit of his life. A better lot, however, was in store for him. A good angel, in the person of Lady Murray, interfered on his behalf. She had been anxiously considering how she could save his life. Her plans were speedily formed, and in the morning she ventured to lay them before her irate husband. As Hogg has humorously described the scene—

The lady o' Elibank raise wi' the dawn,
An' she waukened Auld Juden, an' to him did say,—
"Pray, what will ye do wi' this gallant young man?"
"We'll hang him," quo Juden, "this very same day."

"Wad ye hang sic a brisk an' gallant young heir,
An' has three hamely daughters aye suffering neglect?
Though laird o' the best of the forest sae fair,
He'll marry the warst for the sake o' his neck.

"Despise not the lad for a perilous feat;
He's a friend will bestead you, and stand by you still;
The laird maun hae men, an' the men maun hae meat,
An' the meat maun be had be the danger what will."

The plan thus suggested seemed feasable. It might really be the wisest course to pursue, at least so Sir Gideon was disposed to think, and no time was lost in bringing the matter to an issue. Young Scott was at once brought into the hall, the terms on which his life was to be spared were briefly stated, and he was afforded an opportunity of seeing the young lady whom fortune had thus strangely thrown in his way. One glance sufficed. The features of Sir Gideon's daughter, known to fame as "Muckle-mou'd Meg," were not attractive. The condemned culprit felt that even the gallows was preferable to such an objectionable matrimonial alliance.

"Lead on to the gallows, then," Willie replied,
"I'm now in your power, and ye carry it high;
Nae daughter of yours shall e'er lie by my side;
A Scott, ye maun mind, counts it naething to die."

These were brave words, bravely spoken. Sir Gideon, however, had made up his mind as to the course he meant to pursue, and Willie Scott was at once led forth to make his acquaintance with the "Hanging Tree." But when he drew near and saw the fatal rope dangling in the wind, his courage began to fail him. The prospect was far from inviting, and he pled for a few days respite to think on his sins, "and balance the offer of freedom so kind." But the old laird was inexorable. He simply said to him, "There is the hangman, and there is the priest, make your choice." Thus driven to bay, Willie saw that further parleying would not avail, and so he thought he had better make the best of a bad business. As he thought over the matter, he began to discover certain traits in the young lady's person and character of a more or less pleasing description. He concluded that, after all, he might do worse than wed with the daughter of Elibank.—

"What matter," quo' he, "though her nose it be lang,
For noses bring luck an' it's welcome that brings.

There's something weel-faur'd in her soncy gray een,
But they're better than nane, and ane's life is sae sweet;
An' what though her mou' be the maist I hae seen,
Faith muckle-mou'd fok hae a luck for their meat."

Thus everything ended happily, and young Harden had cause to bless the day he found himself at the mercy of Sir Gideon Murray of Elibank. Seldom, indeed, has Border reiver been so beneficently punished!

An' muckle guid bluid frae that union has flowed,
An' mony a brave fellow, an' mony a brave feat;
I darena just say they are a' muckle mou'd,
But they rather have still a guid luck for their meat.

Such is the tradition, as Hogg has given it in his humourous poem. It goes without saying that the poet has embellished and enlarged the story to suit his own purposes. But the tradition has generally been regarded as having some considerable basis of fact. Satchells, in his History of the Scotts, thus refers to Auld Wat of Harden and his famous son—

"The stout and valiant Walter Scott
Of Harden who can never die,
But live by fame to the tenth degree;
He became both able, strong, and stout,
Married Philip's daughter, squire of Dryhope,
Which was an ancient family,
And many broad lands enjoyed he;
Betwixt these Scotts was procreat,
That much renowned Sir William Scott,
I need not to explain his name,
Because he ever lives by fame;
He was a man of port and rank,
He married Sir Gideon Murray's daughter of Elibank."

The fortunes of other famous reivers have formed the theme of many a stirring ballad. The so-called historical data on which many of these ballads are professedly based, may often, no doubt, be truthfully described as more imaginary than real, nevertheless the picture which the balladist has drawn is often deeply interesting, and subserves an important end by indicating the feeling with which these men and their deeds were usually regarded.

In a history of Border reiving such side-lights as the ballads afford may be profitably utilized.

Maitland, in his celebrated poem on the Thieves of Liddesdale, makes allusion to a well known character who is known to fame as "Jock o' the Syde." He was nephew to the "Laird of Mangerton," and cousin to the "Laird's Ain Jock," and had all the enthusiasm of his race for the calling to which the members of his clan seem to have devoted their somewhat remarkable talents.—

He never tyris
For to brek byris
Our muir and myris
Ouir gude ane guide.

It is said that he assisted the Earl of Westmoreland in his escape, after his unfortunate insurrection with the Earl of Northumberland, in the twelfth year of the reign of Queen Elizabeth. But according to the balladist his career, on one occasion, had well nigh terminated disastrously. In the company of some of his friends he had made a raid into Northumberland. Here he was taken prisoner by the warden, and thrown into jail at Newcastle, there to "bide his doom." He knew that he would not have long to wait. Not much time was wasted in considering the various items of the indictment, more especially when the accused was a well-known thief. "Jeddart justice" was not confined to the small burgh on the Scottish Border. It was as popular, at that time, in England as anywhere else, as many a Scottish reiver has known to his cost. The friends of the prisoner were fully aware that if he was to be saved from the gallows, not one moment must be lost. A rescue party was speedily organized. The laird of Mangerton, accompanied by a few friends— the Laird's Jock, the Laird's Wat, and the famous Hobbie Noble (an Englishman who had been banished from Bewcastle)—started off for Newcastle with all speed, determined to bring the prisoner back with them, quick or dead. To allay suspicion and avoid detection, they shod their horses "the wrang way"—putting the tip of the shoe behind the frog—and arrayed themselves like country lads, or "corn caugers ga'en the road." When they reached Cholerford, near Hexham, they alighted and cut a tree—"wi' the help o' the light o' the moon"—on which were fifteen nogs or notches, by which they hoped "to scale the wa' o' Newcastle toun." But, as so often happened in like circumstances, this improvised ladder was "three ells too laigh." Such trifles, however, rarely ever proved disconcerting. The bold reivers at once determined to force the gate. A stout porter endeavoured to drive them back, but—

"His neck in twa the Armstrongs wrang;
Wi' fute or hand he ne'er played pa!
His life and his keys at once they hae ta'en,
And cast his body ahint the wa'."

The path being now clear they speedily made their way to the prison, where they found their friend groaning under fifteen stones of Spanish iron (nothing short of this would have availed to keep a stark Scottish reiver, fed on oatmeal, within the confines of a prison cell), carried him off, irons and all, set him on a horse, with both feet on one side, and rode off with the fleetness of the wind in the direction of Liddesdale:

"The night tho' wat, they didna mind,
But hied them on fu' merrilie,
Until they cam' to Cholerford brae,
Where the water ran like mountains hie."

Dashing into the stream they soon reached the opposite bank. The English, who were in hot pursuit, when they reached the Tyne, which was rolling along in glorious flood, durst not venture further. They were filled with chagrin when they saw the prisoner, loaded as he was with fifteen stones of good Spanish iron, safe on the other side. They had sustained a double loss. The prisoner was gone, and he had taken his valuable iron chains with him. The land-sergeant, or warden's officer, taking in the situation at a glance, cried aloud—

"The prisoner take,
But leave the fetters, I pray, to me."

To which polite request the Laird's ain Jock replied—

"I wat weel no,
I'll keep them a'; shoon to my mare they'll be,
My gude bay mare—for I am sure,
She bought them a' right dear frae thee."

No Liddesdale reiver was ever likely to part with anything in a hurry, least of all to give it up to an Englishman.

The Armstrongs, almost without exception, were noted thieves. They seem to have possessed a rare genius for reiving. Their plans were generally so well formed, and carried out with such a fine combination of daring and cunning, that the "enemy" almost invariably came off "second best." One of the last, and most noted of this reiving clan, was *William Armstrong*, a lineal descendant of the famous Johnie of Gilnockie, who was known on the Borders by the name of *Christie's Will*, to distinguish him from the other members of his family and clan. He flourished during the reign of Charles I., a circumstance which shows that moss-trooping did not altogether cease at the union of the Crowns. It is related that, on one occasion, Christie's Will had got into trouble, and was imprisoned in the Tolbooth of Jedburgh. The Lord High Treasurer, the Earl of Traquair, who was visiting in the district, was led to enquire as to the cause of his confinement. The prisoner told him, with a pitiful expression of countenance, that he had got into grief for stealing two *tethers* (halters). The eminent statesman was astonished to hear that such a trivial offence had been so severely punished, and pressed him to say if this was the only crime he had committed. He ultimately reluctantly acknowledged that there were two *delicate colts* at the end of them! This bit of pleasantry pleased his lordship, and through his intercession the culprit was released from his imprisonment.

It was a fortunate thing for Lord Traquair that he acted as he did. A short time afterwards he was glad to avail himself of the services of the man whom he had thus been the means of setting at liberty. The story is one of the most romantic on record, and amply justifies the adage that "truth is stranger than fiction." A case, in which the Earl was deeply interested, was pending in the Court of Session. It was believed that the judgment would turn on the decision of the presiding judge, who has a casting vote in the case of an equal division among his brethren. It was known that the opinion of the president was unfavourable to Traquair; and the point was, therefore, to keep him out of the way when the question should be tried. In this dilemma the Earl had recourse to Christie's Will, who at once offered his services to *kidnap* the president. He discovered that it was the judge's usual practice to take the air on horseback, on the sands of Leith, without an attendant. One day he accosted the president, and engaged him in conversation. His talk was so interesting and amusing that he succeeded in decoying him into an unfrequented and furzy common, called the Frigate Whins, where, riding suddenly up to him, he pulled him from his horse, muffled him in a large cloak which he had provided, and rode off with the luckless judge trussed up behind him. Hurrying across country as fast as his horse could carry him, by paths known only to persons of his description, he at last deposited his heavy and terrified burden in an old castle in Annandale, called the Tower of Graham. The judge's horse being found, it was concluded he had thrown his rider into the sea; his friends went into mourning, and a successor was appointed to his office. Meanwhile the disconsolate president had a sad time of it in the vault of the castle. His food was handed to him through an aperture in the wall, and never hearing the sound of human voice, save when a shepherd called his dog, by the name of *Batty*, and when a female domestic called upon *Maudge*, the cat. These, he concluded, were invocations of spirits, for he held himself to be in the dungeon of a sorcerer. The law suit having been decided in favour of Lord Traquair, Christie's Will was directed to set the president at liberty, three months having elapsed since he was so mysteriously spirited away from the sands at Leith. Without speaking a single word, Will entered the vault in the dead of night, again muffled up in the president's cloak, set him on a horse, and rode off with him to the place where he had found him. The joy of his friends, and the less agreeable surprise of his successor, may be more easily imagined than described, when the judge appeared in court to reclaim his office and honours. All embraced his own persuasion that he had been spirited away by witchcraft; nor could he himself be convinced to the contrary, until, many years afterwards, happening to travel in Annandale, his ears were saluted once more with the sounds of *Maudge* and *Batty*—the only notes which had reached him during his long confinement. This led to the discovery of the whole story, but in those disorderly times it was only laughed at as a fair *ruse de guerre*.

The victim of this extraordinary stratagem was Sir Alexander Gibson, better known as Lord Durie. He became a Lord of Session in 1621, and died in 1646, so that the incident here related must have taken place betwixt these periods.

The version of this incident, given in the well, known ballad "Christie's Will," if not so romantic as the foregoing, is certainly more amusing. The balladist represents Lord Traquair as "sitting mournfullie," afraid lest the vote of the Court of Session would make him bare at once of land and living—

"But if auld Durie to heaven were flown,
Or if auld Durie to hell were gane,
Or ... if he could be but ten days stoun ...
My bonnie braid lands would still be my ain.

At this juncture Christie's Will offers his services—

"O, mony a time, my Lord," he said,
"I've stown the horse frae the sleeping loun;
But for you I'll steal a beast as braid,
For I'll steal Lord Durie frae Edinburgh toun."

"O, mony a time, my Lord," he said,
"I've stown a kiss frae a sleeping wench;
But for you I'll do as kittle a deed,
For I'll steal an auld lurdane off the bench."

He lighted at Lord Durie's door,
And there he knocked maist manfullie;
And up and spake Lord Durie sae stour,
"What tidings, thou stalwart groom, to me?"

"The fairest lady in Teviotdale,
Has sent, maist reverent sir, for thee.
She pleas at the Session for her land a' hail,
And fain she would plead her cause to thee."

"But how can I to that lady ride
With saving of my dignitie?"
"O a curch and mantle ye may wear,
And in my cloak ye sall muffled be."

Wi' curch on head, and cloak ower face,
He mounted the judge on a palfrey fyne;
He rode away, a right round pace,
And Christie's Will held the bridle reyne.

The Lothian Edge they were not o'er,
When they heard bugles bauldly ring,
And, hunting over Middleton Moor,
They met, I ween, our noble king.

When Willie looked upon our king,

I wot a frightened man was he!
But ever auld Durie was startled more,
For tyning of his dignitie.

The king he crossed himself, I wis,
When as the pair came riding bye—
"An uglier croon, and a sturdier loon,
I think, were never seen with eye."

Willie has hied to the tower of Græme,
He took auld Durie on his back,
He shot him down to the dungeon deep,
Which garr'd his auld banes gae mony a crack.
......

The king has caused a bill be wrote,
And he has set it on the Tron—
"He that will bring Lord Durie back
Shall have five hundred merks and one."

Traquair has written a braid letter,
And he has seal'd it wi' his seal,
"Ye may let the auld Brock out o' the poke;
The land's my ain, and a's gane weel."

O Will has mounted his bony black,
And to the tower of Græme did trudge,
And once again, on his sturdy back,
Has he hente up the weary judge.

He brought him to the Council stairs,
And there full loudly shouted he,
"Gie me my guerdon, my sovereign liege,
And take ye back your auld Durie!"

Important as this service was, it was not the only one that Christie's Willie rendered to the Earl of Traquair. He was sent, on one occasion, with important papers to Charles I., and received an answer to deliver, which he was strictly charged to place in the hands of his patron. "But in the meantime," says Sir Walter Scott, "his embassy had taken air, and Cromwell had despatched orders to entrap him at Carlisle. Christie's Will, unconscious of his danger, halted in the town to refresh his horse, and then pursued his journey. But as soon as he began to pass the long, high, and narrow bridge that crosses the Eden at Carlisle, either end of the pass was occupied by parliamentary soldiers, who were lying in wait for him. The Borderer disdained to resign his enterprise, even in these desperate circumstances; and at once forming his resolution, spurred his horse over the parapet. The river was in high flood. Will sunk—the soldiers shouted—he emerged again, and, guiding his horse to a steep bank, called the Stanners, or Stanhouse, endeavoured to land, but ineffectually, owing to his heavy horseman's cloak, now drenched in water. Will cut the loop, and the horse, feeling himself disembarrassed, made a desperate exertion, and succeeded in gaining the bank. Our hero set off, at full speed, pursued by the troopers, who had for a time stood motionless in astonishment, at his temerity. Will, however, was well mounted; and, having got the start, he kept it, menacing with his pistols, any pursuer who seemed likely to gain on him—an artifice which succeeded, although the arms were wet and useless. He was chased to the river Esk, which he swam without hesitation, and, finding himself on Scottish ground, and in the neighbourhood of friends, he turned on the northern bank, and with the true spirit of the Borderer, invited his followers to come through and drink with him. After this taunt he proceeded on his journey, and faithfully accomplished his mission."

If Christie's Will may be regarded as the last Border freebooter of any note, it is evident that the peculiar genius of the family to which he belonged survived in full vigour to the end.

But the last of the Armstrongs who paid the penalty of death for his misdeeds was *Willie of Westburnflat*. It is said that a gentleman of property, having lost twelve cows in one night, raised the country of Teviotdale, and traced the robbers into Liddesdale, as far as the house of Westburnflat. Fortunately, perhaps, for his pursuers, Willie was asleep when they came, and consequently without much difficulty they secured him, and nine of his friends. They were tried in Selkirk, and though the jury did not discover any direct evidence against them to convict them of the special fact, they did not hesitate to bring in a verdict of guilty, on the ground of their general character as "notour thieves and limmers." When sentence was pronounced, Willie sprang to his feet, and laying hold of the oaken chair on which he had been sitting, broke it in pieces, and called on his companions who were involved in the same doom, to stand behind him and he would fight his way out of Selkirk with these weapons. But, strange to relate, they held his hands, and besought him to let them *die like Christians*. They were accordingly executed in due form of law. This incident is said to have happened at the last circuit court held in Selkirk.

Willie Armstrong, as he stood under the gallows-tree, might appropriately have sung the lines composed by *Ringan's Sandi*, a relative of his own, who was executed for the murder of Sir John Carmichael, the warden of the Middle Marches—

This night is my departing night,
For here nae langer must I stay;
There's neither friend nor foe o' mine,
But wishes me away.

What I have done through lack of wit,
I never, never can recall;
I hope ye're a' my friends as yet;
Good night, and joy be with you all!

XIV.

UNDER THE BAN.

The Cardinal rose with a dignified look,
He called for his candle, his bell, and his book!
In holy anger, and pious grief,
He solemnly cursed that rascally thief!
He cursed him at board, he cursed him in bed;
From the sole of his foot to the crown of his head;
He cursed him in sleeping, that every night

He should dream of the devil, and wake in a fright;
He cursed him in eating, he cursed him in drinking,
He cursed him in coughing, in sneezing, in winking;
He cursed him in sitting, in standing, in lying;
He cursed him in walking, in riding, in flying;
He cursed him in living, he cursed him in dying!
Never was heard such a terrible curse!
But what gave rise to no little surprise,
Nobody seemed one penny the worse.

The Jackdaw of Rheims.

As might be expected, the existence of such an extraordinary phenomenon as Border reiving did not escape the attention of the Church. Such a peculiar state of affairs could not be regarded with favour, or treated with indifference. It may be said, no doubt, that the continued existence of such an abnormally lawless and chaotic condition of society on the Borders indicated that the ecclesiastical authorities were either singularly inept, or reprehensibly careless. Why was some attempt not made long before to curb the lawless spirit of the Border reivers? With the exception of the "monition of cursing" by Gavin Dunbar, Archbishop of Glasgow, little or nothing seems to have been done by the Church to stem the tide of Border lawlessness.

In dealing, however, with this phase of the question, there are several considerations which ought to be borne in mind. First of all, it ought to be remembered that while Border reiving was carried on with more or less persistence for some hundreds of years it did not attain really portentous dimensions till well on towards the close of the fifteenth century. Prior to the time of the Jameses, the two countries may be said to have been almost constantly at war. Invasion followed invasion, on the one side and on the other, with a kind of periodic regularity. From the time of James I., onwards to the union of the Crowns in 1603, such invasions, at least on the same large and destructive scale, became less frequent; though, in the intervals of peace, the Borderers kept themselves busy harassing and despoiling each other. This period of comparative calm, it may be remarked, is also synchronous with the decadence of Romanism. From the time of Queen Margaret, of pious memory, to the death of Robert III., the Romish Church enjoyed a period of signal prosperity. Abbeys and monasteries, many of them buildings of great architectural beauty, were erected in different parts of the country, and became important centres of moral and religious authority and influence. Whatever opinion may be entertained regarding Romanism, whether regarded from an ecclesiastical or theological standpoint, the majority of fairly unprejudiced students will be ready to admit that the system was, in many respects, admirably adapted to the circumstances of the country at that particular stage of its development. A strong hand was needed to curb and guide the lawless and turbulent factions of which the nation was composed. It is more than doubtful if, under any other ecclesiastical system—bad as things were—the same beneficent results would have been attained.

But powerful as the Romish Church was in the country, in the heyday of its prosperity, it never attained the same undisputed sway in Scotland which marked its history in other countries, especially on the Continent. The reason of this is not difficult to discover, though it must be sought for far back in the religious history of the people. The Celtic

Church, founded by St. Columba, was neither in doctrine nor polity exactly on Roman Catholic lines. It sought in the East rather than in the West, in Ephesus rather than Rome, its ideals of worship and doctrine. Romanism succeeded in establishing itself only after a long and arduous struggle. And when at last victory had been achieved, and the Church in Scotland had been Romanized, it was discovered that while the form had changed, the spirit of the older Church still survived, and when occasion arose, made itself felt in no uncertain manner. There can be no question that the influence of the Celtic Church continued long after the Church itself had passed away. It is a noteworthy fact that neither the rulers of the people, nor those over whom they exercised authority, were prepared to submit implicitly to the dictation of the Romish see. Their obedience to the great temporal head of the Catholic religion was never either servile or unlimited. They were prepared to take their own way in many things, treating often with much indifference the fulminations of their spiritual superiors. Many illustrations of this tendency may be found in the history of the country. On one occasion, for example, William the Lion appointed his chaplain to the Bishopric of St. Andrews. An English monk was chosen by the Chapter to the same office, and thus a complete deadlock was brought about. What was to be done? The ecclesiastical authorities appealed to the Pope, who was indignant when he learned that the authority of the Church was being thus rudely trampled upon. He conferred legatine powers on the Archbishop of York, and the Bishop of Durham, to "direct the thunder of excommunication" against the King in the event of contumacy. But notwithstanding the extreme gravity of the situation the King stubbornly refused to yield. He not only set the papal authority at defiance, but he banished from the country those who dared to yield to the papal favourite.

This is not, by any means, an isolated instance of stubborn and successful resistance to the authority of the Church. The same thing, in other circumstances, occurred again and again, with the result that the terrors of excommunication ceased to be dreaded.

This, of course, was especially the case during the decadent period of the Catholic *regime*. There are numerous indications in the literature of the fifteenth and sixteenth centuries of this weakening of the ecclesiastical authority. The picture which Sir David Lindsay has drawn of the condition of the Church at this period is no mere spiteful exaggeration, but may be accepted as substantially accurate. Nothing could well more clearly indicate how thoroughly the Church had failed to keep in touch with the intellectual life of the nation, or guide and control its moral and spiritual activities.

It was during this period of weakness, almost of total moral collapse, that the Archbishop of Glasgow took it upon him to excommunicate the Border thieves. Had the same vigorous measure been adopted at an earlier period, the result might have been more favourable. As it was, the launching of this ecclesiastical thunderbolt really created more amusement than consternation. It was regarded simply as the growl of a toothless lion. In no circumstances were the Border reivers easily intimidated. Their calling had made them more or less indifferent to the claims alike of Church and State. They had never had much affection for the king, and they had, perhaps, still less for the priest. Having shaken themselves free, to a large extent at least, from the control of the State, they were not prepared to put their neck under the yoke of an ecclesiastical authority which even the best men of the age had ceased to venerate. But the Archbishop felt that he had a duty to discharge, and he applied himself to the task with commendable vigour. It may be well to explain that there are two forms of excommunication—*excommunicatio major* and *excommunicatio minor*. The former mode of excommunication is one of which we in these days happily know nothing, as it can only be effectively carried out with the approval and assistance of the State, which in modern times would never be granted. But the latter form is still common. It has been retained in the Church as a point of discipline, or, to use a well known and significant theological phrase, as a *poena medicinalis*. The major excommunication was a frightful weapon, and might well be dreaded. Those who suffered the greater excommunication were excluded from the Mass, from burial in consecrated ground, from ecclesiastical jurisdiction, and practically from all intercourse with their fellow Christians. They were, in short, handed over body and soul to the devil.

The "Monition of Cursing," issued by the Archbishop of Glasgow against the Border thieves, was ordered to be read from every pulpit in the diocese, and circulated throughout the length and breadth of the Borders. It is a curious document, and will, doubtless, be read with interest, if not with profit. It was expressed in the following terms:—

"Gude folks, heir at my Lord Archibischop of Glasgwis letters under his round sele, direct to me or any uther chapellane, makand mensioun, with greit regrait, how hevy he beris the pietous, lamentabill, and dolorous complaint that pass our all realme and cummis to his eris, be oppin voce and fame, how our souverane lordis trew liegis, men, wiffis and barnys, bocht and redemit be the precious blude of our Salviour Jhesu Crist, and levand in his lawis, ar saikleslie. part murdrist, part slayne, brynt, heryit, spulzeit and reft, oppinly on day licht and under silens of the nicht, and thair takis. and landis laid waist, and thair self banyst therfra, als wele kirklandis as utheris, be commoun tratouris, revaris, theiffis, duelland in the south part of this realme, sic as Tevidale, Esdale, Liddisdale, Ewisdale, Nedisdale, and Annanderdaill; quhilkis hes bene diverse ways persewit and punist be the temperale swerd and our Soverane Lordis auctorite, and dredis nocht the samyn.

"And thairfoir my said Lord Archibischop of Glasgw hes thocht expedient to strike thame with the terribill swerd of halykirk, quhilk thai may nocht lang endur and resist; and hes chargeit me, or any uther chapellane, to denounce, declair and proclame thaim oppinly and generalie cursit, at this marketcroce, and all utheris public places.

"Heirfor throw the auctorite of Almichty God, the Fader of hevin, his Son, our Salviour, Jhesu Crist, and of the Halygaist; throw the auctorite of the Blissit Virgin Sanct Mary, Sanct Michael, Sanct Gabriell, and all the angellis; Sanct John the Baptist, and all the haly patriarkis and prophets; Sanct Peter, Sanct Paull, Sanct Andro, and all haly appostillis; Sanct Stephin, Sanct Laurence, and all haly mertheris.; Sanct Gile, Sanct Martyn, and all haly confessouris; Sanct Anne, Sanct Katherin, and all haly virginis and matronis; and of all the sanctis and haly cumpany of hevin; be the auctorite of our Haly Fader the Paip and his cardinalis, and of my said Lord Archibischop of Glasgw, be the avise and assistance of my lordis, archibischop, bischopis, abbotis, priouris, and utheris prelatis and ministeris of halykirk, I denounce, proclamis, and declaris all and sindry the committaris of the said saikles murthris, slauchteris, brinying, heirschippes, reiffis, thiftis, and spulezeis, oppinly apon day licht and under silence of nicht, alswele within temporale landis as kirklandis; togither with thair part takaris, assistaris, supplearis, wittandlie resettaris of thair personis, the gudes reft and stollen be thaim, art or part thereof, and their counsalouris and defendouris, of thair evil dedis generalie cursit, waryit, aggregeite, and reaggregeite, with the greit cursing.

"I curse thair heid and all the haris of thair heid; I curse thair face, thair ene, thair mouth, thair neise, thair toung, thair teith, thair crag, thair schulderis, thair breist, thair hert, thair stomok, thair bak, thair wame, thair armes, thair leggis, thair handis, thair feit, and everilk part of thair body, frae the top of thair heid to the soill of thair feit, befoir and behind, within and without. I curse thaim gangand, and I curse thaim rydand; I curse thaim standand, and I curse thaim sittand; I curse thaim etand, I curse thaim drinkand; I curse thaim walkand, I curse thaim sleepand; I curse thaim rysand, I curse thaim lyand; I curse thaim at hame, I curse thaim fra hame; I curse thaim within the house, I curse thaim without the house; I curse thair wiffis, thair banris, and thair servandis participand with thaim in thair deides. I wary thair cornys, thair catales, thair woll, thair scheip, thair horse, thair swyne, thair geise, thair hennys, and all thair quyk gude.. I wary thair hallis, thair chalmeris, thair kechingis, thair stabillis, thair barnys, thair biris, thair bernyardis, thair cailyardis, thair plewis, thair harrowis, and the gudis and housis that is necessair for thair sustentatioun and weilfair. All the malesouns and waresouns. that ever gat warldlie creatur sen the begynnyng of the warlde to this hour mot licht apon thaim. The maledictioun of God, that lichtit apon Lucifer and all his fallowis, that strak thaim frae the hie hevin to the deip hell, mot licht apon thaim. The fire and the swerd that stoppit Adam fra the yettis of Paradise, mot stop thaim frae the gloir of Hevin, quhill thai forbere and mak amendis. The malesoun that lichtit on cursit Cayein, quhen he slew his bruther just Abell saiklessly, mot licht on thaim for the saikles slauchter that thai commit dailie. The maledictioun that lichtit apon all the warlde, man and beist, and all that ever tuk life, quhen all wes drownit be the flude of Noye, except Noye and his ark, mot licht apon thame and droune thame, man and beist, and mak this realm cummirles of thame for thair wicket synnys. The thunnour and fireflauchtis that ξet doun as rane apon the cities of Zodoma and Gomora, with all the landis about, and brynt thame for thair vile synnys, mot rane apon thame, and birne thaim for oppin synnys. The malesoun and confusioun that lichtit on the Gigantis for thair oppressioun and pride, biggand the tour of Babiloun, mot confound thaim and all thair werkis, for thair oppin reiffs and oppressioun. All the plagis that fell apon Pharao and his pepill of Egipt, thair landis, corne and cataill, mot fall apon thaim, thair takkis, rowmys. and stedingis, cornys and beistis. The watter of Tweid and utheris watteris quhair thai ride mot droun thaim, as the Reid Sey drownit King Pharao and his pepil of Egipt, persewing Godis pepill of Israell. The erd mot oppin, riffe and cleiff, and swelly thaim quyk to hell, as it swellyit cursit Dathan and Abiron, that ganestude Moeses and the command of God. The wyld fyre that byrnt Thore and his fallowis to the nowmer of twa hundreth and fyty, and utheris 14,000 and 700 at anys, usurpand aganis Moyses and Araon, servandis of God, mot suddanely birne and consume thaim dailie ganestandand the commandis of God and halykirk. The maledictioun that lichtit suddanely upon fair Absolon, rydand contrair his fader, King David, servand of God, throw the wod, quhen the branchis of ane tre fred him of his horse and hangit him be the hair, mot licht apon thaim, rydand agane trewe Scottis men, and hang thaim siclike that all the warld may se. The maledictioun that lichtit apon Olifernus, lieutenant to Nabogodonoser, makand weir and heirschippis apon trew cristin men; the maledictioun that lichtit apon Judas, Pylot, Herod, and the Jowis that crucifyit Our Lord, and all the plagis and trublis that lichtit on the citte of Jherusalem thairfor, and upon Symon Magus for his symony, bludy Nero, cursit Ditius Makcensius, Olibruis, Julianus, Apostita and the laiff of the cruell tirrannis that slew and murthirit Cristis haly servandis, mot licht apon thame for thair cruell tiranny and murthirdome of cristin pepill. And all the vengeance that ever wes takin sen the warlde began for oppin synnys, and all the plagis and pestilence that ever fell on man or beist, mot fall on thaim for thair oppin reiff, saiklesse slauchter and schedding of innocent blude. I dissever and pairtis thaim fra the kirk of God, and deliveris thaim quyk to the devill of hell, as the Apostill Sanct Paull deliverit Corinthion. I interdite the places thay cum in fra divine service, ministracioun of the sacramentis of halykirk, except the sacrament of baptissing allanerllie; and forbiddis all kirkmen to schriffe or absolve thaim of thaire synnys, quhill. they be first absolyeit of this cursing. I forbid all cristin man or woman till have ony cumpany with thaime, etand, drynkand, spekand, prayand, lyand, gangand, standand, or in any uther deid doand, under the paine of deidly syn. I discharge all bandis, actis, contractis, athis, and obligatiounis made to thaim be ony persounis, outher of lawte, kyndenes or manrent, salang as thai susteine this cursing; sua that na man be bundin to thaim, and that thai be bundin till all men. I tak fra thame and cryis doune all the gude dedis that ever thai did or sall do, quhill thai ryse frae this cursing. I declare thaim partles of all matynys, messis, evinsangis, dirigeis or utheris prayeris, on buke or beid; of all pilgrimagis and almouse dedis done or to be done in halykirk or be cristin pepill, enduring this cursing.

"And, finally, I condemn thaim perpetualie to the deip pit of hell, to remain with Lucifeir and all his fallowis, and thair bodeis to the gallowis of the Burrow Mure, first to be hangit, syne revin and ruggit with doggis, swyne and utheris wyld beists, abhominable to all the warld. And thir candillis gangis frae your sicht, as mot. thair saulis gang fra the visage of God, and thair gude fame fra the warld, quhill thai forbeir thair oppin synnys foirsaidis and ryse frae this terribill cursing, and mak satisfaction and pennance."

XV.

THE TRIUMPH OF LAW.

'Tis clear a freebooter doth live in hazard's train,
A freebooter's a cavalier that ventures life for gain,
But since King James the Sixth to England went,
There's been no cause of grief or discontent,
And he that hath transgressed the law since then,
Is no freebooter but a thief from men.

    Satchell.

hen we turn our attention to the study of the causes which ultimately resulted in the abolition of Border reiving, we find that this desirable end was brought about, to a considerable extent at least, by a change of environment. Conditions were gradually created which made the old system not only undesirable, but unnecessary, both from a political and economic point of view. An important step was taken when Buccleuch, at the instigation of "the powers that be," drafted off large numbers of the "broken men" to the Belgic wars. In the campaigns which were then being conducted in the Low Countries, these hardy, valiant Borderers no doubt gave a good account of themselves; but, so far as can be ascertained, few of them ever returned to "tell the tale." Still more drastic measures were adopted in order to get rid of the Græmes, who inhabited the Debateable land, and whose depredations had provoked a bitter feeling of resentment on both sides of the Border. It seemed hopeless to expect any improvement in their habits so long as they were allowed to remain where they were, and so they were banished from the country, shipped across the channel to the Emerald Isle, where it is to be hoped they found a congenial sphere, and sufficient scope for their abilities. Perhaps in course of time they settled down to a more orderly, if less exciting, mode of life than that to which they had hitherto been accustomed.

But, notwithstanding the removal of these lawless men from the Borders, it was found that those who had been left at home were either unwilling or unable to abandon their reiving habits. The disease had long been chronic, and those responsible for the government of the country began to realise that the cure was not to be effected in any

105

instantaneous fashion. Time and patience were alike necessary in order to the successful accomplishment of the end desiderated. The task of restoring order, more especially in the Liddesdale district, was committed to the able hands of the "Bold Buccleuch." When he returned from abroad he was invested with the most arbitrary powers to execute justice on the malefactors, and he went about his work in the most resolute and business-like manner. Well known thieves were apprehended and immediately put to death. There were no prisons to lodge them in, and as it would have been, in most cases, a sheer waste of time to subject them to any form of trial—most of them being well known depredators who gloried in their crimes—they were executed without ceremony. In this way large numbers of the worst characters were disposed of, and a wholesome fear created in the minds of those who were fortunate enough to escape the gallows. If Buccleuch, in his rash and impetuous youth, was responsible for much of the mischief done on the Borders, he amply atoned for his indiscretions by the splendid services he now rendered to the State in suppressing lawlessness, and inaugurating, in this distracted region, the reign of law and order. His name will remain indissolubly associated with one of the most eventful and stirring periods in Border history, and we feel certain that the fame of his prowess will not suffer from a more minute acquaintance with the varied incidents of his remarkable career.

But the main factors in the social and moral regeneration of the Borders were—

(1) The Union of the Crowns.

(2) The Planting of Schools.

(3) The Restoration of the Church.

This order may not represent, and we do not think it does represent, the relative value of the influences which produced the radical and significant change which now took place in the habits and life of the people on both sides of the Border. But it will best suit our purpose to consider these agencies in the order stated.

For a period of wellnigh four hundred years it had been the ambition of successive English monarchs to reduce Scotland to a state of vassalage. From the time of Edward this object was never altogether lost sight of. Again and again the project seemed on the eve of accomplishment, but some untoward event always occurred to render the scheme abortive. Doubtless, had the union of the Crowns taken place at an earlier period, both countries would have escaped some unpleasant and regrettable experiences. There can be no doubt that the hostility which marked the relationships of the two nations, had—at least from an economic point of view—an injurious effect on the people of Scotland. Industry in all its branches was crippled by the constant turmoil which prevailed. The Scottish kings, moreover, were "cribb'd, cabin'd, confin'd" by the ambitions and jealousies of a turbulent and factious nobility, who, in their relations to the State, were too frequently dominated by unpatriotic and selfish motives. Had it been possible for the sovereign to lay a strong hand on his nobles, and compel them to pay more regard to imperial interests than to their own private ends and petty jealousies, all might have been well. But such a course was often practically impossible. The barons were all powerful within their own domain, and when it served their purposes they seldom hesitated even to usurp the authority of the king. This abnormal condition of affairs made the government of the country a matter of extreme difficulty, and gave rise to endless trouble and vexation. No doubt it may legitimately be argued that, painful as this state of matters undoubtedly was, it was after all better that the Scottish nation should have retained its independence, with all the drawbacks attaching thereto, than that it should have conceded the demand of England for annexation. The difficulties of the situation were the making of the people. This may be frankly admitted. But, at the same time, it was a good thing for the country when at last the Scottish king ascended the English throne, and became the ruler of both nations. A new era was thus inaugurated, an era of progressive wellbeing in nearly every department of national life.

It is worthy of note that, for a few years before James succeeded to the throne of England, his feeling towards the Scottish Borderers had become considerably modified. Whether this was due to the influence of the reproachful letters on the state of the Borders addressed to him by Elizabeth, or to the additional subsidy of £2000 per annum, now guaranteed to him out of the English exchequer, is a question about which there may, legitimately, be difference of opinion. In any case he now saw that it would be advantageous, from a personal as well as from a national point of view, to curb as far as he possibly could the lawless propensities of the reiving fraternity. In so doing he was wisely anticipating the time when he would be responsible for good rule on both sides of the Border. It may thus be said that even the prospect of the union of the Crowns under James had a beneficial effect. Coming events cast their shadows before. It led to the adoption of a wiser policy in regard to this particular part of the realm, with the result that for some years prior to 1603, a noticeable improvement had taken place in Border affairs. The wardens had become more anxious than before to discharge the duties of their high office with impartiality, and to use their utmost endeavour to restrain the more lawless spirits among the clansmen over whom they exercised authority. Crime was at once more expeditiously and severely punished. A firm hand was laid on the ringleaders in Border strife; and though these men were not easily daunted, and chafed bitterly under the restraints laid upon them by those in authority, yet they were soon made to realise that a new spirit was being infused into the administration, and that in consequence reiving was becoming an increasingly difficult and perilous business. But great social revolutions are not brought about in a day; and, as we shall see, it was long ere the Borders settled down into their present normal condition.

When James ascended the throne of England, the change which had been silently taking place in the management of Border affairs became at once more marked and widespread. The effect of this event was unmistakable in every department of the national life. It created, no doubt, considerable bitterness and jealousy in certain sections of society in England, as it was believed that the King was unduly partial to his own countrymen in the bestowment of his favours. This was certainly not the case, as James was far more anxious to conciliate his English subjects than to favour his native land. It would have been well for him, and his successors in office, had he discharged his duty to Scotland with less regard to English prejudices.

He was determined, however, at all hazards to suppress Border reiving. Ten days after his arrival in London he issued a proclamation requiring all those guilty of *the foul and insolent outrages* lately committed on the Borders, to submit themselves to his mercy before the twentieth of June, under penalty of being excluded from it for ever. Two days after this proclamation had been made he emitted another, declaring his fixed resolution to accomplish the union of the two realms; in consequence of which, the bounds possessed by the rebellious Borderers should no more be the *extremities* but the *middle*, and the inhabitants thereof reduced to a perfect obedience. He said that he had found in the hearts of his best disposed subjects of both realms, a most earnest desire for this union; and he undertook, with the advice and consent of the Estates of both Parliaments, to bring it about. In the meantime he declared that he considered the two kingdoms as *presently united*; and required his subjects to view them in the same light, and in consequence thereof, to abstain from mutual outrages and injuries of whatever kind, under the penalty of his highest displeasure and of suffering the strictest rigour of justice.

In pursuance of this policy, and in order to extinguish all past hostilities between his kingdoms, the King prohibited the name of *Borders* any longer to be used, substituting in its place the name *Middleshires*. He also ordered all the places of strength, with the exception of the habitations of noblemen and barons, to be demolished; their iron gates to be converted into ploughshares; and the inhabitants were enjoined to betake themselves to agriculture and other works of peace.

But these severe measures, accompanied as they were by the summary execution of large numbers of the worst characters on the Borders, who, as we have seen, were sent to the gallows without ceremony, would not have been sufficient of themselves to eradicate the evil. More potent influences, however, were brought into operation. The law was now administered, not spasmodically as before, but with a continuity and impartiality hitherto unknown and unattainable. It was the interest of the King and of the Government to repress disorder, to punish the lawless and disobedient, and to establish order and good rule throughout both kingdoms; and the consequence was that, in course of time, the Border reivers were made to realise that they must, perforce, abandon their old habits and betake themselves to a new mode of life. This desirable end was not attained without difficulty. Border reiving did not altogether cease for nearly a hundred years after the union of the Crowns; but the beginning of the seventeenth century inaugurated the period of its decline.

"The succession of James to the Crown of England," Ridpath remarks, "and both kingdoms thus devolving on one sovereign, was an event fruitful of blessing to each nation. The Borders, which for many ages had been almost a constant scene of rapine and devastation, enjoyed, from this happy era, a quiet and order which they had never before experienced; and the island of Britain derived from the union of the two Crowns, a tranquility and serenity hitherto unknown, and was enabled to exert its whole native force. National prejudices, and a mutual resentment, owing to a series of wars betwixt the kingdoms, carried on for centuries, still however subsisted, and disappointed James' favourite scheme of an entire and indissoluble union. From the same source also arose frequent disputes and feuds upon the Marches, which by the attention of the sovereign were soon and easily composed; and are not of moment enough to merit a particular relation. But it required almost a hundred years, though England and Scotland were governed all the time by a succession of the same princes, to wear off the jealousies and prepossessions of the formerly hostile nations, and to work such a change in their tempers and views, as to admit of an incorporating and an effectual union."

But another and most important agent in the pacification and social regeneration of the Borders was the development, under the fostering care of the Church, of what is known as the Parochial system of education. The Roman Catholic Church in earlier times was not, as has sometimes been erroneously supposed, inimical to the intellectual culture of the nation. In its palmy days it undertook the work of educating the people with an enthusiasm which commands the respect of most unbiased students of our national history.

In this respect the monasteries, especially, rendered important services to the community. Long before the Reformation there were at least three classes of schools in Scotland—the "Sang Schools," connected with the Cathedrals or more important Churches—the "Grammar Schools," which were founded in the principal burghs in the country—and the "Monastic Schools," which were, as the name implies, connected with the monasteries. "The interest in education," says Prof. Story, "which had distinguished the Columban Church, was not seriously impaired by its amalgamation with the Church of Rome. It survived in active force, and before the foundation of any of the existing public schools of England (the oldest of which is Winchester, founded in 1387), we find the charge of the schools of Roxburghshire intrusted in 1241 to the monks of Kelso, over whom was an official called 'The Rector of the Schools.'"

But for a considerable period prior to the Reformation, the interest of the Roman Catholic Church in education, as well as in regard to the moral and spiritual well-being of the people, had become enfeebled. The monasteries had ceased to be, what they were in earlier times, centres of gracious intellectual and spiritual influence. And nowhere was this more conspicuously the case than on the Borders. The lawlessness of the clans reacted on the life of the Church, and instead of the Church overcoming the malign and disintegrating influences by which it was assailed, it was unhappily overcome by them. Education in all its branches was shamefully neglected. The most eminent barons in the land were often unable even to write their own names. When they were under the necessity of adhibiting their signatures to deed or charter, the pen had to be guided by the hand of the notary. In these circumstances it is not difficult to imagine how densely ignorant the great body of the people must have been.

Whatever may be said for or against the Reformation, there will be a general consensus of opinion, among educationists especially, that the scheme propounded by John Knox for the education of the people is in many respects an ideal one. It is thus outlined in the Book of Discipline:—"Of necessitie therefore we judge it, that every several kirk have one schoolmaister appointed, such a one at least as is able to teach grammar and the Latin tongue, if the town be of any reputation. If it be upland where the people convene to the doctrine but once in the week, then must either the reader or the minister there appointed take care of the children and youth of the parish, to instruct them in the first rudiments, especially in the Catechism as we have it now translated in the Book of Common Order, called the Order of Geneva. And furder, we think it expedient, that in every notable town, and specially in the town of the superintendent, there be erected a Colledge, in which the arts, at least logick and rhetorick, together with the tongues, be read by sufficient masters, for whom honest stipends must be appointed. As also that provision be made for those that be poore, and not able by themselves nor by their friends to be sustained at letters, and in special these that come from landward."

Unfortunately, owing to the rapacity of the nobles, this splendid scheme of national education was not carried out in its entirety. But though the enlightened views which the Reformers thus endeavoured to impress both upon the Parliament and the country were not so heartily and widely adopted as they should have been, a beginning was made in the establishment of parochial schools, and by this means the benefits of education were brought within the reach of the great body of the people. It has been justly remarked that if the counsel of the Reformers had been followed, no country in the world would have been so well supplied as Scotland with the means of extending the benefits of a liberal education to every man capable of intellectual improvement.

The state of the Borders, however, for at least fifty years after the Reformation, was such as to make it difficult in some places, and all but impossible in others, to establish and maintain parochial schools. But in course of time, as things began to improve, owing to the more systematic and impartial administration of the law, the work of training the youth of the district was entered upon with energy and enthusiasm. The beneficial results of the new regime in matters educational soon became apparent. Crime steadily decreased. The old reiving habits were gradually, if with difficulty, abandoned, and increased attention was given to the peaceful pursuits of agriculture and other industries; and out of the social chaos which had so long been a notorious feature of Border life, a healthy, vigorous, law-abiding community was evolved.

But the most potent factor in the pacification and moral regeneration of the Borders was the influence and teaching of the Church. The religious condition of the people in this part of the country, both before and after the Reformation, can only be described as utterly deplorable. The fierce fighting Border clans had practically broken with institutional religion in all its forms. It is frequently said of them, and not without good reason, that they feared neither God nor man. They delighted in robbing and burning churches, and held both priest and presbyter in high disdain. Johnie Armstrong of Gilnockie is credited with having destroyed, during the course of his career, no fewer than fifty-two parish churches. The picture of the religious condition of the Borders, as reflected in the State Papers, is well fitted to awaken painful reflections. Eure, for example, in a letter addressed to Queen Elizabeth, in the year 1596, says:—"Another most grievous decay is the 'want of knowledge of God,' whereby the better sort forget oath and duty, let malefactors go without evidence, and favour a partie belonging to them or their friends. The churches mostly ruined to the ground, ministers and preachers 'comfortless to come and remain where such heathenish people are,' so there are neither teachers nor taught." In a still more doleful strain the Bishop of Durham describes the irreligious condition of the Borders. "Diverse persons," he says, "under pretext of danger to their persons, and some through a careless regard of their conscience toward their flocks, besides also other out of a continual corruption of their patrons, turn residence into absence, whereby the people are almost totally negligent and ignorant of the truth professed by us, and so the more subject to every subtile seducer.". So completely, indeed, had religious teaching fallen into abeyance that one writer even goes the length of affirming that "many die, and cannot say the Lord's Prayer."

The Commission appointed to inquire into the state of affairs on the Borders, after the breaking of Carlisle castle by Buccleuch, and to discover, if possible, some remedy for the clamant evils which prevailed, suggested in the first paragraph of their report "that ministers be planted at every Border Church to inform the lawless people of their duty, and watch over their manners—the principals of each parish giving their prime surety for due reverence to the pastor in his office; the said churches to be timely repaired."

The propriety and wisdom of this deliverance will not be seriously questioned by those who have some knowledge of the motives and principles by which human life is moulded and governed. Religion is the bulwark of society and the State—the necessary condition alike of their existence and wellbeing. It was therefore clearly perceived by those responsible for the social and moral wellbeing of this much distracted region that some effective measures must be adopted to revive the religious life of the people. The task was none of the easiest. Ruined churches had to be restored; ministers had to be found, and "honest stipends" provided; and the community from an ecclesiastical point of view reorganized. And, as might be expected, the changes contemplated were not easily or quickly effected. Old habits are not readily abandoned, and consequently it took many years to raise the general religious life of the Borders to the level of that of other districts of the country where the conditions, to begin with, were more favourable. Even in the beginning of the eighteenth century, when that renowned minister, the Rev. Thomas Boston, began his pastorate in Ettrick, the state of matters from a religious point of view was such as might well have appalled the stoutest heart. His parishioners were rude and lawless to a degree. We are told that on Sundays some of them went, not to church, but to the churchyard, and tried to drown the voice of the preacher by producing all sorts of discordant sounds; and even those who ventured within the walls ostensibly to worship, would rise up during the service with "rude noise and seeming impatience," and leave the building. The condition of this parish—and others in the district were probably not much better—has been not inaptly described as "an unploughed field covered with tangled weeds and thorns, and sheltering many foul creatures." But the morals of the people, under the influence of the faithful ministrations of Boston, were gradually reformed, and the desert was made to bud and blossom like the rose. And what was effected in this particular district may be taken as a fair sample of the good work accomplished by the Church throughout the whole length of the Borders. Its influence was potent and far-reaching, and mighty to the pulling down of the strongholds of evil. "How did it happen,"

110

says a modern writer, "that the raiding and reiving race which inhabited the Borders became so peaceful and law-abiding? That were a long tale to tell, but the credit of it belongs to those preachers Sir Walter was too superfine and cavalier to understand. In this work his own great-grandfather, for nineteen years the faithful and diligent minister of Yarrow, bore his own part, and, though the great-grandson owed his genius to his mother, the minister's grand-daughter, he failed to appreciate the most characteristic treasure of his inheritance. He remembered that Richard Cameron—founder of the Cameronians, sternest of Presbyterian sects—was once chaplain to the Harden Scotts, but he could see no heroism in the uncompromising preacher, who had dared to rebuke Harden's too compliant faith and indulgent temper. Yet over Annandale, throughout Moffatdale, thence flowing over into the Forest, the name of Cameron was one of power. The heroic strain in him suited the mood of the ancient reivers, who loved strength and iron in the blood. But the Scotts had ridden and lorded it over the Marches too long to love iron in any blood save their own. Their feud with the preachers began early, for John Welsh, Knox's son-in-law, was persecuted out of Selkirk, whither he had gone to convert the souters and reform the freebooters of the Forest, by a Scott of Headshaw. But the man who ought here to be placed foremost is a man who became minister of Ettrick three years before John Rutherford, Scott's ancestor, died—Thomas Boston. Cotter Morrison quoted some of his fierce sayings with the horror of a son of light suddenly confronting an altogether incredible darkness. But no man ignorant of the deeds of Boston can judge his speech. In some of his words there is a wonderful tenderness, in his acts a marvellous integrity, and in his thought a rare power to move the hearts, stir the consciences, and awaken the intellects of his people. It was a brave thing to make the stern Presbyterian discipline a reality among these men of the Forest, in whom the old reiving instinct was still strong, at once kept alive and glorified by the ballads which were known in every cottage, and recited at every hearth. But the man was patient and strong enough to do it; nothing was too minute to escape his eye; nothing was too inveterate to silence or too ancient to overcome his religion." It is undoubtedly to the influence of such preachers, men of faith and character, scholarship and genius, that Borderers owe many of the best qualities, both of intellect and heart, for which, in later times, they have become distinguished.

XVI.

THE HARVEST OF PEACE.

When this loose behaviour I throw off,
And pay the debt I never promised,
By how much better than my word I am,
By so much shall I falsify men's hope;
And, like bright metal on a sullen ground,
My reformation, glittering o'er my fault,
Shall show more goodly, and attract more eyes,
Than that which hath no foil to set it off.

Shakespeare.

T o those familiar with the history of Border reiving it may appear, on the first glance, somewhat inexplicable that in those districts where the system was most deeply rooted there should now be found one of the most orderly and law-abiding communities in the country. The old leaven, it would seem, has worked itself out, and that, too, with a rapidity and thoroughness which some may find difficult to reconcile with the modern doctrine of heredity. The laws of evolution, whether in the physical or social sphere, may operate with the precision and certainty of destiny, but the changes effected are brought about slowly, and with well-graded regularity. No doubt fifty or a hundred years is a considerable period measured by the standard of the individual life, but it is a brief term in the history of a nation or people. While considerable changes may take place in the course of a century, yet these are often of a more or less superficial character, affecting only to a limited extent the thoughts, habits, and customs of a community. In the present instance, however, the changes which took place in the life of the Border clans seem to have been as thorough as they were rapid. In a comparatively short time the Borders, from being one of the most lawless and disorderly districts in the country, became an example to both kingdoms in honesty, sobriety, and true patriotism. Such epithets as "brutal Borderers" and "lewd Liddesdales," so freely banded about in earlier times, especially by the English wardens, speedily lost their significance. Those lawless reivers, whom neither warden nor king could effectively control, were not difficult to induce, when the proper time came, to turn their swords into ploughshares and their spears into pruning hooks, and to settle down to a well-ordered, industrious, and peaceful mode of life. This phenomenon may doubtless be accounted for on purely natural principles. The explanation, indeed, is not difficult to discover. As we have already seen, the worst characters, the "broken men"—those who had no chiefs who could be made responsible for their good behaviour—were expatriated—sent to Holland and elsewhere—and consequently ceased to give further trouble. And it may be said in regard to those who remained that while they had spent the best part of their lives in appropriating the goods and chattels of their English neighbours, they were not by any means the depraved and degraded wretches they have so often been described. Far from it. These men for the most part believed, rightly or wrongly, that in despoiling and harassing their English neighbours they were rendering an important service to their country. They looked upon their reiving as being of the nature of reprisal. Time and again they had been hunted and harried by their "auld enemies," and they thought it no sin, whenever they found an opportunity, to carry the war into the enemies' camp. Moreover, it seems to have been an article of their creed—one of the "fundamentals"—that all property was common by the laws of nature, a doctrine which, even at the present day, is sometimes propounded with considerable show of logic by budding Border politicians. Their ethical system was simplicity itself. Might was right. The spoil belonged by natural law to the man who could either take or keep it. Of course it may be said that such notions are opposed to the foundation principles of all social and moral life. This may be conceded. But the fact that the Border reivers looked at things from a different point of view—while it may not mitigate the offence abstractly considered—had an important bearing and influence on their own moral life and character. There can be no doubt that it saved them from utter demoralization. He that doubteth is damned. But the Borderers were fully convinced that their action in plundering and despoiling those who lived in the opposite Marches was commendable and right. Johnie Armstrong may be taken as a faithful exponent of Border ethics when he says:—

For I've loved naething in my life,
I weel dare say it, but *honesty.*

He leaves us in no doubt as to what he means by the assertion. He does not deny that he took everything he could lay his hands on from the unfortunate English. He glories in the fact. It never occurs to him that he ought to feel ashamed of his conduct. But he avers that though he had lived for a hundred years never a Scot's wife could have said that "ere he had skaithed her a puir flee." It was right to rob the English; it was disgraceful to turn your hand against anyone belonging to your own country. Here we have the ethical system of the Border reiver in a nutshell.

But lawless as the Borders may have been in the olden time, they certainly do not at the present day bear many traces of their evil past. The Border counties, judging from the statistics of the Police and Sheriff Courts, have an excellent record, whether we consider the number or the nature of the cases dealt with. The following statistics speak for themselves:—

County.	Population.	Average Number of Convictions for the last five years.		
		M.	F.	Total.
Selkirk	10,101	315	37	352
Roxburgh	34,537	589	105	694
Berwick	32,406	287	56	343
Dumfries	61,274	539	74	613
Peebles	14,761	284	41	325

But these statistics would appear still more favourable were it not for the existence of what is known as the "Tweed Act," which is responsible for a considerable proportion of the crime charged against the Border counties. In the county of Peebles, for example, fully 17 per cent. of the convictions recorded are under this exceptional statute. It is a law which is often fiercely denounced both by poachers and politicians, and of which few others have much that is kindly to say, with the exception perhaps of the riparian proprietors; but no really serious attempt has as yet been made to have the Tweed and its tributaries brought under the general law of the land. But notwithstanding the existence of this fruitful source of crime, the Borders compare not unfavourably with other districts. The population of Caithness, for instance, is only a little over 4000 higher than that of Berwick, and we find that the average number of convictions in that county for the past five years is 419, a fact which shows that the inhabitants of the south are quite as well conducted as those in the far north.

It is also worthy of note that the offences dealt with are for the most part of a petty nature. There are comparatively few cases of theft, or offences against the person. It may therefore be said that the Borders have emerged from the evil conditions of the past, bearing few traces, if any, of their former lawlessness. It was no doubt a hard school in which Borderers were trained, and, perhaps, as has been remarked, some of them are a trifle grim, and dour, and unsociable, deficient to some extent in the softer and kindlier virtues characteristic of the inhabitants of the western seaboard; but, considering the experiences through which they have passed, they have no reason to be ashamed of themselves.

And if Borderers have deficiencies arising out of the adverse circumstances with which they had so long to contend, they have also outstanding excellencies which have brought them well to the front in the race of life. They are brave, outspoken, independent. They think and act with energy and decision. They believe in themselves, rely upon their own resources, and where the struggle is most severe they almost invariably give a good account of themselves. Their contributions in modern times to the social and intellectual life of the nation have been considerable, and of a high quality. In agriculture, in commerce, in statesmanship, in warfare, and in many other departments, they have rendered important services. The Scotts and Kers and Elliots—names intimately associated with Border reiving in all its phases—have long held a foremost place in the political and social life of the country.

But the great feature of Border life in more modern times has been the almost marvellous efflorescence of the spirit of poesy, which has conferred on the district a unique distinction and an imperishable charm. It may seem strange that the home of the reiver should have become the birthplace of poetry and song; yet a moment's reflection will suffice to show that here are to be found all the conditions which make life a tragedy and beget the feeling for it. The rough adventurous life of the Border reiver, with its constant peril and hairbreadth escapes, formed, as it were, a fitting compost for the cultivation of the tragic muse. And what ballads have sprung from this soil watered by the very heart's blood of its people! "The Dowie Dens of Yarrow," "The Douglas Tragedy," "Johnie Armstrong," "Jamie Telfer of the Fair Dodhead," "The Border Widow's Lament," "The Flowers of the Forest"—not to mention many others of almost equal merit—have taken possession of the imaginative and emotional life of the nation, and become part and parcel of its very being. Indeed, the influence of this varied body of balladic lore on the thought and life and character of the Scottish people can hardly be over-estimated. Spenser, to whose sublime genius we are indebted for the "Faery Queen," is known to fame as "the poet's poet." It is a high distinction, and not unworthily bestowed. But in a still higher sense it may be said that the Border ballads have been a perennial fountain of poetic inspiration to all lovers of the Muse. Rough and rugged though many of them are, yet they are dowered with that potent spell which at once captivates the heart and awakens within it the deepest and tenderest emotions of which it is capable. Here, if anywhere, we find the Helicon of Scotland.

We may regret, with R. L. Stevenson, that the names of the old balladists have disappeared from the roll of fame. It would have been interesting to know who the singers were; but we may be thankful that the songs they sung have come down to our later age. They are a priceless inheritance, a glorious legacy. In these ballads the rugged cactus of Border life has burst into the most gorgeous blossom.

But this is not all. The ballad period, rich as it is in all the higher elements of dramatic and poetic suggestiveness, was but the beginning of an era of song, which has secured for the Borderland an unique distinction. In the beginning of the eighteenth century there was born in the manse of Ednam, in the neighbourhood of Kelso, one of the most renowned of Border poets, James Thomson, the author of "The Seasons," "The Castle of Indolence," "Rule Britannia," and other pieces. His early youth was spent in the parish of Southdean, and here among the green rolling hills, and by the quiet streams, he stored his mind and imagination with those images of natural beauty which in later times, in a far-off city, he embodied in immortal verse. His services to the poetic literature of his age and country have been tardily, and often very inadequately, appreciated. To him mainly belongs the credit of bringing the minds of men back to nature and reality as the only genuine sources of poetic inspiration. He was the forerunner of Cowper, and Burns, and Wordsworth—the pioneer in a new and profoundly significant movement.

After a considerable interval, Scott, Hogg, and Leyden appear on the scene—names that will for ever remain enshrined in Border song and story. Scott was a Borderer of Borderers, a descendant of Auld Wat of Harden and Mary Scott, the Flower of Yarrow. His grandfather, on the maternal side, was Professor Rutherford, a famous man in his day, the scion of an old Border stock, renowned, like the Harden family, in the annals of reiving.

Hogg and Leyden occupy a place of honourable distinction in the life and literature of the Borders. "Kilmeny" is a masterpiece of imaginative genius, and has won for its author a fame which the lapse of time will not seriously impair. John Leyden, more renowned as a scholar and antiquary than a poet, gave evidence of the possession of powers which, had he been spared, would have secured for him a foremost place among the most brilliant men of his age. These services which the Borders have thus rendered to the literature of the country have been valuable and important in a high degree.

And—if we dare suggest it—it is not altogether improbable that even Burns himself was sprung of a Border stock. We find in the "Border Papers," from which much of our information regarding Border reiving has been drawn, that the name "Burness" frequently occurs. The family bearing this patronymic was well known in Liddesdale and the Debateable land, and the various branches of the family, like the Armstrongs and Elliots, were distinguished for their reiving propensities. The grandfather of the poet found a home in Argyleshire, and Burns' father, as is well known, hailed from Kincardineshire. The removal from the Borders of a representative of the family may be easily accounted for. Reference has already been made to a law which was passed by the Scottish Parliament enacting that the various families and clans on the Borders should find pledges for their good behaviour. These "pledges" were sent north of the Forth, and were strictly prohibited from returning to their former haunts. It is just possible that in this way an ancestor of Burns may have been called to leave the Border district in the interests of his family or clan. This much at least is certain, the name is one which was common on the Borders in those times of which we write. But whatever truth there may be in the suggestion we have made (it would be foolish to dogmatise in the absence of authentic information), Burns furnishes many points of resemblance to the distinctive traits of Border character in the olden time. His disregard of conventionality in all its forms, combined with his aggressive sense of independence, mark him out as of the true Border type.

This district, once so famous as the favourite haunt of the reiver, may now be described as one of the most peaceful in the country. Every year it attracts an increasing number of tourists, who come from almost every part of the world to visit its numerous shrines. To the literary and professional classes it has become a kind of Mecca, to which they feel constrained to resort once and again for intellectual refreshment and inspiration. The glamour which Scott, Wordsworth, and Hogg—and many other tuneful poets—have thrown around its green hills and bosky glens has given it an air of enchantment to which the poetic temperament especially is keenly sensitive. The pity is that in modern times, owing to a variety of causes, the population in the rural districts has been steadily decreasing. The fine hardy, thrifty, yeomen race is disappearing. Small holdings have been consolidated, and the big farm—in too many cases—is held by a non-resident tenant, who interests himself little, or not at all, in the social and moral well-being of those whom he is under the necessity of employing. This evil is one of long standing. In the Statistical Account of Yarrow, published in 1833, Dr Russell remarks that—"out of forty-five farms in the parish, twenty are *led* farms. On many of these were formerly large families, with servants and cottagers, and there are five such lying adjacent,—a state of things the more to be regretted, when its only advantage is a trifling addition of rent, and the saving of outlay on farm buildings." Well may it be said—

"Ill fares the land, to hastening ills a prey,
Where wealth accumulates, and men decay:
Princes and lords may flourish, or may fade,
A breath can make them, as a breath has made:

But a bold peasantry, their country's pride,
When once destroyed, can never be supplied."

CPSIA information can be obtained at www.ICGtesting.com
Printed in the USA
BVOW06s0132101215

429915BV00013B/74/P